Access 2002

Level 1

Marilyn Campbell

Access 2002: Level 1

Part Number: 084400
Course Edition: 2.2

Acknowledgments

Project Team

Curriculum Developer and Technical Writer: Marilyn Campbell • **Development Assistance:** Jan Mater-Cavagnaro • **Copy Editor:** Angie J. French • **Technical Editor:** Elizabeth M. Swank • **Technical Development Assistance:** Kathy Donovan • **Print Designer:** Daniel P. Smith

NOTICES

HELP US IMPROVE OUR COURSEWARE

Your comments are important to us. Please contact us at Element K Press LLC, 1-800-478-7788, 500 Canal View Boulevard, Rochester, NY 14623, Attention: Product Planning, or through our Web site at **http://support.elementkcourseware.com.**

This logo means that this courseware has been approved by the Microsoft® Office Specialist Program to be among the finest available for learning Microsoft Access 2002. It also means that upon completion of this courseware, you may be prepared to take an exam for Microsoft Office Specialist qualification.

What is a Microsoft Office Specialist? A Microsoft Office Specialist is an individual who has passed exams for certifying his or her skills in one or more of the Microsoft Office desktop applications such as Microsoft Word, Microsoft Excel, Microsoft PowerPoint, Microsoft Outlook, Microsoft Access, or Microsoft Project. The Microsoft Office Specialist Program typically offers certification exams at the "Core" and "Expert" skill levels. The Microsoft Office Specialist Program is the only program in the world approved by Microsoft for testing proficiency in Microsoft Office desktop applications and Microsoft Project. This testing program can be a valuable asset in any job search or career advancement.

To learn more about becoming a Microsoft Office Specialist, visit **www.microsoft.com/officespecialist**. To learn more about other Microsoft Office Specialist approved courseware from Element K, visit **www.elementkcourseware.com**.

*The availability of Microsoft Office Specialist certification exams varies by application, application version, and language. Visit **www.microsoft.com/officespecialist** for exam availability.

ACCESS 2002: LEVEL 1

CONTENTS

LESSON 7: CREATING AND USING REPORTS

APPENDIX A: MICROSOFT OFFICE SPECIALIST PROGRAM

ABOUT THIS COURSE

This course is for the new user of Access and assumes no experience with relational databases. The topics cover the critical skills you need to get started creating databases in Access and working with the data by using tables, queries, forms, and reports.

Access, like other relational database management systems, is not easy to learn all on your own. There are concepts and theories about relational databases that are essential to working with these data repositories. Even if you will only be using a database created by someone else, understanding how a database is designed and structured will make your work easier and help you troubleshoot any data problems you might encounter. Almost all users of Access need to create queries, forms, or reports, and this course will get you started.

Course Description

Target Student

This course targets people who want to gain the skills necessary to use Access to create a database to hold information on a subject and/or the basic skills needed to maintain and report on data in an Access database.

Course Prerequisites

To ensure your success, we recommend you first take the following Element K course or have equivalent knowledge:

- *Windows 2000: Introduction*

How to Use This Book

As a Learning Guide

Each lesson covers one broad topic or set of related topics. Lessons are arranged in order of increasing proficiency with *Microsoft Access*; skills you acquire in one lesson are used and developed in subsequent lessons. For this reason you should work through the lessons in sequence.

We organized each lesson into results-oriented topics. Topics include all the relevant and supporting information you need to master *Microsoft Access*, activities allow you to apply this information to practical hands-on examples.

You get to try out each new skill on a specially prepared sample file. This saves you typing time and allows you to concentrate on the skill at hand. Through the use of sample files, hands-on activities, illustrations that give you feedback at crucial steps, and supporting background information, this book provides you with the foundation and structure to learn *Microsoft Access* quickly and easily.

As a Review Tool

Any method of instruction is only as effective as the time and effort you are willing to invest in it. In addition, some of the information that you learn in class may not be important to you immediately, but it may become important later on. For this reason, we encourage you to spend some time reviewing the topics and activities after the course. For additional challenge when reviewing activities, try the "What You Do" column before looking at the "How You Do It" column.

As a Reference

The organization and layout of the book makes it easy to use as a learning tool and as an after-class reference. You can use this book as a first source for definitions of terms, background information on given topics, and summaries of procedures.

Course Objectives

In this course, you will practice the critical skills necessary to create a database and enter, find, edit, and report on the data it contains.

You will:

- define the purpose of and terminology associated with a relational database and Access objects.
- follow the steps required to properly design a database.
- create tables to hold data and then establish table relationships.
- modify the design of and work with data in tables.
- create, modify the design of, and work with select queries.
- create and modify forms to work with your data.
- create and modify reports to select, organize, and print data.

Course Requirements

Hardware

- Pentium 133 MHz or higher processor required for all operating systems.
- 64 MB of RAM recommended minimum for Windows 2000 Professional; in addition, you should have 8 MB of RAM for each application running simultaneously.
- 600 MB of free hard-disk space. (Under Windows 2000, at least 4 MB of space must be available in the Registry.)
- Either a local CD-ROM drive or access to a networked CD-ROM drive for the installation of the software and course data files.
- A two-button mouse, an IntelliMouse, or compatible pointing device.
- VGA or higher-resolution monitor; Super VGA recommended.

Software

- A complete installation of Microsoft Office XP Professional.
- An installed printer driver.

Class Setup

This book was written using the Windows 2000 Professional operating system. Using this book with other operating systems may affect how the activities work.

To set up the student workstations, complete the following steps:

1. Install Windows 2000 Professional on a newly formatted hard drive.
2. If the Getting Started With Windows 2000 window is displayed, uncheck Show This Screen At Startup and click Exit.
3. Install a printer driver.
4. Perform a complete installation of Microsoft Office XP Professional.

   The steps above need to be done only once. The following steps must be done before every class to ensure a proper setup.

5. On the student's computers, reset the usage data. (Open Access, then choose Tools→ Customize and click Reset My Usage Data to restore the default settings).
6. On each student workstation, log in as the student, and extract the data files to the My Documents folder.

LESSON 1

Working with a Relational Database

Lesson Objectives:

In this lesson, you will define the purpose of and terminology associated with a relational database and Access objects.

You will:

- Identify the uses of a relational database.
- Associate terms with the objects used in a relational database.
- Use a template to create a new Access database.
- Examine the objects created to see if they meet your information needs.

Introduction

Many of us have large amounts of data that we need to record and track, and a relational database is the best way to organize most collections of information. In fact, we are surrounded by databases today, and the use of databases continues to grow. For customer records, inventory, and personalized Web sites, a database is the preferred tool.

In this lesson, you'll become acquainted with the terms used in working with databases in Microsoft Access. You will see an example of an Access database, and you will also create a new database by using an Access Wizard.

Knowing what a relational database is and how to create and work with one in Access is a very valuable skill. You'll be able to organize data that is important to your job and will be able to maintain more accurate data. You'll also save time and work.

TOPIC A

Identify Uses of a Relational Database

This topic will help you identify a database and determine when you should use one. It is the first step on your journey to working with Access.

In order to be able to work with databases, you first need to know one when you see one, and then be able to figure out when Access is the best tool for the task you need to accomplish. This topic will help you with these decisions.

What is a Database?

Definition:

> A *database* is a collection of related information or data. A database of information can be on paper or on a computer; it is merely a set of facts or data that are related in some way.

Example:

> Common examples of databases are phone books, medical and financial records, personnel information, mailing lists, and dictionaries.

DISCOVERY ACTIVITY 1-1

Identifying Databases

Scenario:

Imagine that you have a very curious eight-year old child who seems to know as much as or more than you do about computers. He comes home from school one day after studying about the U.S. Census and asks you what a database is. You'd like to be able to give him an explanation.

1. What are some examples of sets of data that you use in your personal life?

2. What are some examples of collections of data you use in your job?

3. What are some other examples of collections of data that you encounter daily?

Identify Uses of a Relational Database

A *relational database* is one in which the data is stored in a structure of rows and columns, usually called tables. An electronic relational database management system is the implementation of this structure in a computer software application such as Access 2002.

Guidelines

The power of a relational database application lies in its ability to store and manipulate large amounts of data. It enables you to:

- Sort data. You can view data in many ways without affecting the data that is stored. For example, from a company's personnel database, you could produce a list of employees according to their hire dates.

- Extract data. You can select specific information to view, modify, or print, by using criteria to extract just the data you want. For example, you might want to print a list of employees who work in one specific department.

- Summarize data. You can perform calculations on numeric data. For example, you could produce a list or report that shows totals or averages for all records or a group of records.

Example:

A relational database software application such as Access 2002 is best suited for storing and working with lists of related data. So, for example, information like names, addresses, and records—such as customer orders and personnel and payroll data—are best maintained in Access.

Non-Example:

Software applications are designed to serve a specific purpose. Microsoft Word is an excellent word-processing application and can be used to compose letters, memos, newsletters, reports, and other documents that consist mostly of text. Microsoft Excel is a spreadsheet application that is best used for working with financial and other numeric information such as budgets; it is not intended to store large amounts of data.

DISCOVERY ACTIVITY 1-2

Identifying Appropriate Software Applications

Activity Time:

5 minutes

Scenario:

You work for The Greene Supply Co., a fictitious company that sells environmentally safe home care products. It's a small company and you're playing catch-up in the age of computerization and nobody in the company knows a lot about computers. You've expressed your willingness to learn so you've just been appointed head of the new Information Management department. Your first assignment is to help department managers determine when Access is the best tool for the tasks they need to accomplish.

For each of the following situations, indicate whether or not Access would be the appropriate choice.

1. _____ The VP of Finance needs to analyze potential profits for a new product line.

2. _____ The Customer Service manager wants to be able to handle customer orders and invoices electronically.

3. _____ The President of the company needs to prepare the annual report.

4. _____ The head of sales and marketing wants to create a list of customer names, addresses, and buying preferences for use in targeted mailings.

TOPIC B

Define Database Terminology

Part of learning any new discipline is understanding the language that's used. Now that you know what a database is and when to use one, in this topic, you'll be introduced to the dialect of databases.

If you took a job as a golf caddy, but didn't know what a putter was, you probably wouldn't be too successful. In order to work with Access databases successfully, you need to know what various terms refer to.

Define Database Terminology

In Access 2002, the following terms are used.

Term	Meaning	Example
table	A group of records stored in rows and columns	Records holding names and addresses
record	A set of data about one person or thing	The name and address of one person
field	A category of information that pertains to all records	Phone numbers
value	A single piece of data	The phone number contained in one record

DISCOVERY ACTIVITY 1-3

Defining Terminology

Scenario:

You're meeting with the President of The Greene Supply Co. to try to explain why you think much of the company's information needs to be stored in relational databases. She's unfamiliar with databases and needs help understanding the terminology and developing a mental picture of what you mean when you talk about data tables. So you decide to draw her an illustration.

1. In the data table given below, circle and label an example of each of the following elements.

___ field   ___ record

___ value

LastName	FirstName	Address	City	State	ZipCode
Abbott	Rob	107 6th St.	Holley	OH	72234
Atkinson	Angela	1012 Main St.	Fairville	IN	80221
Ballantyne	Carl	62 Crescent Ave.	Lyons	OH	72245
Barefoot	Karen	866 Colonial Dr.	Charter	IN	80219
Barnett	Amy	4772 S. Union	Lyons	OH	72247
Cardinale	Alex	12 Cooper Dr., Apt. 2B	Holley	OH	72235
McMillan	Lynne	270 Lima Rd.	Dustin	OH	72308
Nguyen	Tram	45 Oak Dr.	Charter	IN	80219
Sudore	Carrie	5299 Decker Rd.	Holley	OH	72234
Wang	Amy	43 East Ave.	Fairville	IN	80221

TOPIC C

Create a New Database Based on a Template

You've acquired a lot of terms but may be wondering what an Access database looks like and how it works. The next logical question is "How do I create my own database?" This topic will show you an example database and one method of creating a new database.

You may have an occasion when building a database fast is more important to you than having a database that is specifically tailored to your needs. In this topic, you'll have the opportunity to see the database templates that Access provides and to use the Database Wizard.

Access Objects

The various components of an Access database are referred to as *objects*. So, for example, each table that stores data is an object. The other types of objects that you will work with in this course are in the following table.

Object	Purpose
query	Retrieves specific fields and/or records from one or more tables
form	Enables you to view, enter, and edit data in a format similar to a paper form
report	Enables you to arrange data in a format suitable for printing

The Database Window

The Database window in Access (see the example in Figure 1-1) displays and gives you access to the various objects contained in the database. It also enables you to run various wizards and other commands and functions.

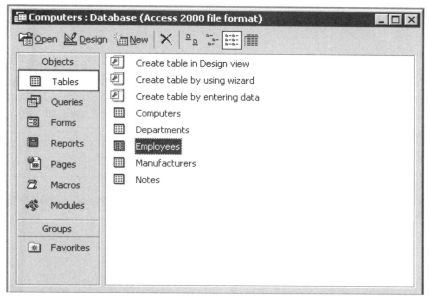

Figure 1-1: *An example of the Database window.*

Access Database Formats

The default file format for databases created in Access 2002 is the Access 2000 format. This enables you to share the database with Access 2000 users without having to convert it. Databases created with Access 2000 can be opened and used in Access 2002 without conversion. Databases created in a version of Access earlier than 2000 should be converted to version 2000 and then, possibly, to 2002.

You might want to use the Access 2002 file format if you:

- Do not need to share the database with users of any other version of Access.
- Want the database to be compatible with any future versions of Access.
- Want to take advantage of the improved storage format of version 2002.

Datasheet View

Datasheet view is the default view of data from a table or a query with the data arranged in rows and in columns. It resembles the appearance of an Excel worksheet.

The Relationships Window

The Relationships window in Access provides a graphical representation of the tables in a database and the relationships you have established between those tables. It also enables you to enforce referential integrity in the relationship between tables and select other options pertinent to table relationships.

INSTRUCTOR ACTIVITY 1-4

Exploring an Access Database

Data Files:

- Computers.mdb

Scenario:

You've convinced the President of The Greene Supply Co. that you need to set up a number of databases. You've done a lot of research on relational database management systems and are trying to decide between using Microsoft Access and another product. You've asked a vendor to come in to show you a demonstration of exactly how Access could be used in your company—so sit back and relax while you're given a tour.

What You Do	How You Do It
1. **Run Access and open Computers** from the My Documents folder.	a. **Choose Start→Programs→Microsoft Access.**
	b. **Click Open** 📂 .
	c. If necessary, in the Places bar, **select My Documents.**
	d. In the file list, **select Computers.mdb.**
	e. **Click Open.**
2. **Examine the Database window.** The title bar displays the name and format of the database. The Objects bar is on the left. The Tables button is selected and the tables in the database are displayed. This example database holds an inventory of a company's computers and includes information about the employees to whom they are assigned.	
3. **Open the Employees table.**	a. In the list of tables, **double-click on Employees.**

4. Observe the Employees table.

    What is this view of the data called?

    What fields of data are included in this table?

---

5. Close the Employees table and open the EmployeeComputers form.

    a. **Click on the Close button** [×].

    b. In the Objects bar, **select Forms.**

    c. In the list of forms, **double-click on EmployeeComputers.**

---

6. How might you use this form?

---

7. Close the EmployeeComputers form and open the DepartmentalComputers report.

    a. **Click the Close button.**

    b. In the Objects bar, **select Reports.**

    c. In the list of reports, **double-click on DepartmentalComputers.**

    d. If necessary, **maximize the Print Preview window.**

    e. If necessary to enlarge the preview to 100%, **place the mouse pointer over the report until it becomes a magnifying glass and click on the report.**

---

8. What information is given in this report?

---

9. Close the report preview and open the query AdminEmployees.

    a. On the Print Preview toolbar, **click Close** [Close] .

    b. In the Objects bar, **select Queries.**

    c. In the list of queries, **double-click on AdminEmployees.**

---

10. **What data does this query provide?**

_____

11. **Close the query datasheet.**   a. In the query's Datasheet window, **click the Close button.**

12. **Match the type of Access object with the description of the function(s) that it performs.**

___	report	a.	Display data for editing.
___	table	b.	Arrange data for printed output.
___	query	c.	Display selected data.
___	form	d.	Store data on a single topic.

13. **One more stop on the tour. Open the Relationships window.**   a. **Choose Tools→Relationships.**

14. **What do you use the Relationships window for?**

_____

15. **Close the Relationships window and close the Computers database.**

a. In the Relationships window, **click the Close button.**

b. In the Database window, **click the Close button.**

Create a New Database Based on a Template

Procedure Reference: Create a New Database Based on a Database Template

To create a new database based on a database template:

 Depending on the speed and capacity of your computer, it may take the wizard 30 minutes or more to build a database based on a template. You will be unable to use Access during that time.

1. Start Access.

2. If necessary, click New to display the New File task pane.

3. In the New File task pane, under the New From Template heading, click on the General Templates link.

4. In the Templates dialog box, select the Databases tab.

5. Click on the template you wish to use.

6. Click OK.

7. In the File New Database dialog box, navigate to the folder in which you wish to store the database file.

8. In the File Name text box, enter the name for the file.

9. Click Create.

10. Click Next.

11. For each table that the template provides, select any optional fields that you wish to include.

12. Click Next.

13. Select the style you want for forms in the database and click Next.

14. Select the style you want for printed reports and click Next.

15. If you want the title of the database to be different from the file name, enter that title. Click Next.

16. If you do not want the database to be opened after the wizard builds it, uncheck Yes, Start The Database. If you want help on using a database, check Display Help On Using A Database. Click Finish.

Task Panes

Task panes are provided for several common functions in Access and are displayed automatically on the right side of the screen. The New File task pane is displayed by default when you start Access.

Templates

Access provides several *templates* on which you can base a new database. The template provides a database designed to hold a certain type of data (such as Order Entry or Resource Scheduling). A basic set of templates is installed on your computer when you install Access and additional templates are available on the Microsoft Web site through a link provided on the New File task pane.

File Name and Title

Access databases are stored in a MDB file. When you create a new database, you assign a name to this file.

The title of a database is the name that is displayed in the title bar of the Database window. The title can be the same as the file name or you can give it a different and, perhaps, more descriptive title.

ACTIVITY 1-5

Creating a New Database Based on a Template

Scenario:

You've decided on Microsoft Access as your relational database management system. You liked the example of a computer inventory database that the vendor demonstrated for you and decide you'd like to make that your first database project. You'd also like to show the company President results as soon as possible, so you decide you'll try creating the database using a template provided by Microsoft.

What You Do	How You Do It
1. In Access, **create a new database based on the Asset Tracking template. Name the database file** *My Computers* **and save it in the My Documents folder.**	a. If necessary, **choose Start→Programs→ Microsoft Access.**

 You might have a shortcut to Microsoft Access on your desktop and can double-click on that to run Access.

 By default in Office XP applications, the Language bar is displayed in the top-right area of the screen when you first open an application. You can remove it from the screen by right-clicking on the Language bar and choosing Close Language Bar.

b. If Access has already been started and a database opened, the New File task pane is not displayed. **Click New** (or choose File→New) to display the New File task pane.

   If you just started Access, the New File task pane is already displayed.

c. In the New File task pane, under the New From Template heading, **click General Templates.**

d. In the Templates dialog box, **select the Databases tab.**

e. **Select the Asset Tracking template.**

f. **Click OK.**

g. In the File Name text box, **type** *MyComputers*.

h. If necessary, in the Places bar, **select My Documents.**

i. **Click Create.**

2. **What are the types of information the database will store?**

3. Continue with the wizard and review the fields that will be included for each table. Accept the default list of tables and the required fields.

   a. Click Next.

   b. With the Asset Information table selected in the left pane, **scroll through the right pane** to view the list of fields.

   c. **Select the next table listed in the left pane and scroll through the right pane to view the fields.**

   d. **Repeat for each table in the list.**

   e. When done, **click Next.**

4. Preview the form styles, and then select the Standard style and continue with the wizard.

   a. To preview a style, **select the name of the style in the list.**

   b. **Select the Standard style.**

   c. **Click Next.**

5. Now you can choose a report style. Preview the various styles before selecting the default Corporate style and continuing with the wizard.

   a. To preview a report style, **select the name of the style in the list.**

   b. **Select the Corporate style.**

   c. **Click Next.**

6. The title of the database is what is displayed in the title bar of the Database window and is often the same as the file name. **Assign a title of *MyComputers* and continue with the wizard.**

   a. In the text box, **type *MyComputers*.**

   b. **Click Next.**

7. The final screen asks if you want to open the database after the wizard builds it. Since the wizard takes a long time to run and we've provided the completed database, **cancel the wizard.**

     It takes 30 minutes or more for the Database Wizard to create a complete database, and you cannot open another database during that time. For the purpose of class, you'll bypass that wait by cancelling out of the wizard and opening the completed database that has been provided for you.

a. **Click Cancel.**

TOPIC D

Examine the New Database

You've used a template and the Database Wizard to create a new database the fast and easy way. Now you need to see if you think you might be able to use this database to actually track your inventory of capital assets.

Using a template to create a new database takes less time and effort than building your own database from scratch. But, as with any off-the-shelf solution, it may not meet your needs. This is your opportunity to take a look.

Examine the New Database

A database should contain only the objects you need to hold data related to the subject of the database. A database should not contain unnecessary tables and tables should not contain unnecessary fields.

Guidelines

When creating a database, be careful **not** to include:

*   Unnecessary tables
*   Unnecessary fields

Example:

If the purpose of your database is to hold employee information, it should contain only related tables and fields. It should not, for example, contain a table with customer order data.

Switchboard

Some builders of databases, including the Database Wizard, create a form referred to as a *Switchboard*. A Switchboard form usually contains command buttons that enable the user to access the various objects in the database. It is tailored specifically for the database and can serve as an alternative to the Database window as a home base for the user.

AutoNumber Field

A field with a data type of *AutoNumber* is a special type of field in Access. As you enter a new record, Access automatically enters a sequential and unique number, starting with a value of 1, in this field.

ACTIVITY 1-6

Examining the New Database

Data Files:

- Asset Tracking.mdb

Scenario:

Creating a new database using the wizard was pretty painless. But will you actually be able to use the database to track your computer inventory? Before you show it to the company President, you'd better take a look and see if you think it will work for you.

What You Do	How You Do It
1. Now you'll open a copy of the database generated by the wizard. From the My Documents folder, **open the Asset Tracking database.** Notice that this database opens with a Main Switchboard—a form that provides buttons to assist the user. The Database window is minimized in the bottom-left corner of the Access window.	a. **Click Open** 🖼️ . b. **Verify that My Documents is selected in the Places bar.** c. In the list of files, **select Asset Tracking.** d. **Click Open.**
2. **Open the form that enables you to Enter/View Assets and view the fields. Close the Assets form and open the form to Enter/View Other Information.**	a. **Click Enter/View Assets.** b. **View the fields on the form.** c. **Click the Close button.** d. **Click Enter/View Other Information.**

3. Use this Form Switchboard to open the various data entry forms. View the fields on each form.

   a. Click Enter/View Employees.

   b. Click the Close button.

   c. Open, examine, and close each of the data entry forms.

4. Are the fields in this database a match for the data you want to track?

5. Return to the Main Switchboard form and see what Preview Reports provides.

   a. Click Return To Main Switchboard.

   b. Click Preview Reports.

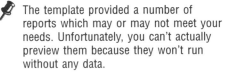 The template provided a number of reports which may or may not meet your needs. Unfortunately, you can't actually preview them because they won't run without any data.

6. Now take a look at the actual database objects. **Return to the Main Switchboard and restore the Database window. Display the list of tables.**

   a. **Click Return To Main Switchboard.**

   b. In the Database window, **click the Restore button**

   c. In the Objects bar, **click Tables.**

7. The only way to have a database that exactly meets your requirements is to design and build it yourself so that's where we're headed. **Close the Asset Tracking database.**

   a. In the Database window, **click the Close button.**

Lesson 1 Follow-up

Good work! You have learned the basics of working with a relational database. You also know when to use a relational database. You can identify the objects in a database and you understand how they interact. You know how to create a database using a template and you can identify areas that need improvement due to template restrictions. You're ready to begin making plans for building a database from scratch.

1. Why is it important to understand the way the database objects interact?

2. What kinds of information do you plan to build databases for?

NOTES

LESSON 2
Planning a Database

Lesson Time
60 minutes

Lesson Objectives:

In this lesson, you will follow the steps required to properly design a database.

You will:

- Define the scope of a new database.
- Use existing resources to help identify what data is needed.
- List the necessary fields.
- Decide what tables are needed by logically grouping the fields.
- Apply database design principles to eliminate potential data maintenance problems.
- Designate a primary key for each table and, where applicable, a foreign key.
- Identify the relationship between data in tables.

Introduction

Now you're familiar with database terminology. You've also seen that using a template may not precisely meet your needs, or there may not be a template that's appropriate for the information you need to maintain. So there will be times when you'll need to create your own database from scratch. You might be tempted to sit down at your computer, run Access, and start creating tables. But, just as you wouldn't attempt to build a house without a blueprint, you can't create a database without a plan.

If the tables and table relationships in a database are not designed properly, the data can be inaccurate or take more work to maintain. For instance, in the example table shown in Figure 2-1, the department name is repeated for each employee in that department. So, if a department name changed, you would have to edit it in multiple records—increasing the chance of error. As much as possible, you want to store a piece of data in one place.

DeptName	EmployeeLastName	EmployeeFirstName	AssetTag	Manufacturer
Administration	Ballantyne	Carl	1250	Omni
Administration	Barnett	Amy	1043	Omni
Administration	Coleman	William	1215	Omni
Administration	Greene	Allison	1020	HiTech
Administration	Middlebrook	Rachel	1072	Cyber
Finance	Brown	Andrea	1052	Cyber
Finance	Nguyen	Tram	1199	Cyber
Fulfillment	Elmore	Heather	1042	Omni
Fulfillment	Haygood	Eric	1044	Micron
Fulfillment	McMillan	Lynne	1075	Omni
Fulfillment	Smith	Jason	1164	Cyber
Fulfillment	Wang	Amy	1198	Atlas
Fulfillment	Wang	Amy	1066	HiTech

Figure 2-1: *An improperly designed table.*

Using this same example table, if you wanted to add a new employee who was not assigned a computer, the new record would have blanks in the fields about the computer. Blank values usually indicate an improperly designed table. Also, if an employee left the company and you deleted his or her record, you would also be deleting information about a computer—which is probably not what you would want to do.

If you decided you also wanted to record the name of each department's manager and added a field to do that, you would introduce many blank values. A properly designed database enables you to change the design as your information needs change or grow and, thus, will save you time and effort.

TOPIC A

Identify Database Purpose

The first step in the design process is to determine what purpose you want the database to serve.

A clear statement of purpose for a new database defines its scope and helps to guide your design. If you start thinking about tables for data not related to the purpose of the database, the statement of purpose will help get you back on track.

Designing a Relational Database

There is a standard procedure that is used to design relational databases and that's the procedure you'll use in this lesson. The steps follow.

Procedure Reference: Design a Relational Database

This procedure may look like a lot of work, but, just like with your new house, you can't start putting up the walls until you've built the foundation. This procedure ensures that your database will comply with relational database design principles, like a review of house blueprints makes sure it complies with building and zoning codes.

1. Identify the purpose of the database.

2. Review existing data.

3. Make a preliminary list of fields.

4. Organize the fields into tables.

5. Enter sample data, review for possible data maintenance problems (this is known as data *normalization*), and revise the table design as necessary.

6. Identify primary and foreign keys.

7. Identify relationships between the data in tables.

8. Finalize the design.

Statement of Database Purpose

A clear statement of purpose for a new database defines its scope and helps to guide your design. If you start thinking about tables for data not related to the purpose of the database, the statement of purpose will help get you back on track. The statement of purpose defines the boundaries of the database; it is sometimes useful to include a statement of what the database will **not** do.

Identify Database Purpose

A database should hold only related information. A properly designed relational database should contain only the data necessary to support the specific purpose of the database. It should not contain tables that are not related to the purpose and, therefore, not related to the other tables.

For example, if you were going to create a new database to track the enrollment of employees in benefit plans, the statement of purpose might be *"The database will contain information on employees and benefit plan enrollment. It will not duplicate information already contained in the payroll information database."*

If your statement of purpose is something like *"The database will track customer orders, employee information, and the company's computer inventory,"* the scope of the database is too large. The data would not all be related and probably require three different databases.

DISCOVERY ACTIVITY 2-1

Writing a Statement of Purpose

Scenario:

In your new position as head of Information Management for The Greene Supply Co, you've decided you want to create a custom database to track your company's computers and what employees they are assigned to.

1. Given the preceding scenario, write a statement of purpose for the new database.

TOPIC B

Review Existing Data

Now that you know what you intend the database to do, you can start thinking about what data it will have to contain to fulfill that purpose. This is the second step in the design procedure.

You can get a real jump-start on knowing what data you need by looking at what data already exists. Is there any relevant data that is now collected and filed on paper forms? Or is someone already tracking some of it in a spreadsheet? Not only will this help identify data you'll want to include in your database, you may find that some of it exists in electronic form that you can import rather than re-entering it.

Review Existing Data

The best way to begin identifying fields for your database is to see what data is already recorded. The database designer needs to get a lot of detail and make a lot of decisions along the way. When looking at existing data, make sure you understand its meaning and find out whether it is consistently available.

Business Rules

The procedures and policies of a company represent its business rules, and these can affect the design of a database. For example, if your company has an internal policy that computers are assigned to departments, rather than to specific employees, this would impact the way you design your tables. As you look at existing data, if you don't already know the pertinent company policies, you should inquire about them.

DISCOVERY ACTIVITY 2-2

Reviewing Existing Data

Scenario:

The statement of purpose for your database is "The database will hold information on the company's inventory of computers and their assignment to employees."

In your search for existing data, you find that the Receiving department fills out a ticket, as shown in Figure 2-2, for each item that is delivered.

The Greene Supply Co.

Receiving Department

Date: _06/30/01_

Item: _Omni desktop computer system_

Notes: _assigned Asset tag # 1266_

For: _Sales department_

Figure 2-2: *The Receiving ticket.*

1. Given the statement of purpose and the existing data shown in Figure 2-2, list the fields you think you will need to include in the database.

Employee Name *Name of Computer* *Type of Computer* *Asset tag#* *dept Assigned* *Date assigned*

TOPIC C
Determine Fields

From reviewing the existing data, you've got a good start on your field list. You can complete step 3 in the design procedure by questioning potential users of the data about their expectations and, specifically, what reports or summary information they would like. You can then reverse-engineer that into specific fields of data.

You don't want to spend a lot of time creating a database and designing beautiful forms and reports only to find out that they don't meet the needs of the consumers of the information. You can prevent this by involving these people in the design and getting as much detail as possible about their information needs.

Determine Fields

An additional technique for gathering specifications for your database is to ask potential users of the data what reports or summary information they would like to see.

Guidelines

When designing a database, be sure to ask potential users:

- What sort of data they expect the database to contain.
- What kinds of reports they require.
- What types of summary information they would like to see.

Example:

If, for example, the manager of each department says they would like to get a list of the computers assigned to them, you won't be able to extract that data unless you have a field that identifies the department. If the company President would like a report that shows the total spent on computer hardware each quarter, you can't produce that report without the supporting data.

DISCOVERY ACTIVITY 2-3

Completing the List of Fields

Scenario:

So far, you've arrived at the following list of fields:

- Employee name
- Date received
- Employee department
- Asset tag number
- Description
- Note

Now, you've completed interviews with all the potential users of the computer inventory information. The manager of Technical Services would like to get a daily report of all new computers received and to whom they are assigned so she can arrange to set up the hardware; she would also like to know if the system is covered by a warranty. The Finance manager would like a monthly summary of departmental computer hardware purchases.

1. **Given the scenario above, list any additional fields you will need in the database.**

add Warranty   Purchase price

TOPIC D *organize*

Group Fields into Tables

Once you've identified the fields you need in the database, you move on to step 4 of the procedure and decide how to organize them into tables. That's what you'll work on next.

Tables are the heart of your database. They're the objects that actually store your data and are what you use as the basis for queries, forms, and reports. While you can change the design of tables after they're created, it's much less work to try and get the right table design at the start.

Group Fields into Tables

Each table in your database should hold information on **one** subject. At this point in the design process, don't be concerned about having too many tables. It's much more likely that you won't have enough.

Guidelines

Think of a table subject as a collection of logically related information with common characteristics. A table should hold information on only one subject.

Example:

If you were creating a database to hold information about the operation of your ice cream stand, you might have an IceCream table. If you sold sundaes as well as cones, you might have a Toppings table. Then, to associate ice cream and toppings in particular combinations and record prices, you might have a Sundaes table.

 If five different database designers followed the recommended design process for the same database, it is entirely possible they would arrive at five slightly different designs. This is because each individual can have a different thought process and may make different assumptions along the way. That's why the standard design process is so important. It helps ensure that, whatever the details of the final design, it will comply with good design principles.

Field and Table Names

Access 2002 has the following constraints on field and table names:

*   No more than 64 characters.

*   Cannot include a period (.), exclamation point (!), an accent grave ('), brackets ([]), or double quotation marks (").

*   Cannot have a leading space. (Access permits you to have spaces within table and field names; however, if there is an internal space, you will have to enclose that table or field name within brackets when you refer to it in expressions and other places. So, you might want to get in the habit of not using spaces in table and field names.)

Names should be brief but descriptive so that another user will know what they mean. Table names are usually plural.

DISCOVERY ACTIVITY 2-4

Deciding on Tables

Scenario:

You're continuing work on designing your computer inventory database and you've decided that you need the following fields:

- Employee name
- Employee department
- Asset tag number
- Manufacturer
- Note
- Date received
- Warranty coverage
- Purchase price

---

1. **Using the previous field list and following the guidelines on naming fields and tables, list the tables you'll need with the fields that each will contain.**

Employees
EmployeeName
Department

Computers
AssetTag
Manufacturer
Note
DateReceived
Warranty
PurchasePrice

TOPIC E

Normalize the Data

Once you've drafted the tables and fields you believe you need in your database, the next step is to enter some sample data in the tables and look for any potential problems with maintaining the data.

Identifying possible data maintenance problems before you enter your real data and start working with your database will save you many headaches and extra work later on. Improperly designed tables can also result in inaccurate data, and you certainly don't want to be making decisions based on data that you can't trust.

Normalize the Data

Data normalization ensures that when you implement the tables you design in Access or another relational database management system, they will work correctly.

Guidelines

Data normalization guidelines are as follows:

- Each field should contain the smallest meaningful value.
- There should be no repeated groups of fields (similar data belongs in the same field).
- There should be no unnecessarily repeated data values.
- All fields in a table should pertain to every record (no blank data values).

Example:

A table containing the following fields would comply with the data normalization guidelines:

- Employee First Name
- Employee Last Name
- Street Address
- City
- State
- Zip Code

Non-Example:

A table containing the following fields would violate these data normalization guidelines.

- Employee Name
- Department
- Project 1
- Effort 1
- Project 2
- Effort 2

- Spouse

Blank Values

In a properly designed table, there should be blank values in fields only because that value is temporarily missing or unknown—not because that field does not pertain to a record. So, for example, if you have a table listing employees that contains a WebSite field, that field would contain a blank value for some employees (assuming that not everyone has a Web site). The value isn't temporarily missing or unknown; the field just doesn't apply to every record. That's a sign that the field belongs in a separate table.

Denormalize Data

After a database designer has fully normalized the design of a database, he or she may, on occasion, choose to *denormalize* a portion of the design. This means that the designer might decide to combine data into one table that the normalization process indicated should be in two tables. This is sometimes done for performance reasons, such as making queries run faster against very large tables.

DISCOVERY ACTIVITY 2-5

Normalizing Data

Scenario:

Before you look at the tables for your computer inventory database, you'll look at some sample tables that are constructed specifically to illustrate the major and most common data maintenance problems caused by the improper design of tables.

1.

LastName	FirstName	Address
Abbott	Rob	107 6th St., Holley, OH 72234
Ballantyne	Carl	62 Crescent Ave., Lyons, OH 72245
Barefoot	Karen	866 Colonial Dr., Charter, IN 80219
Sudore	Carrie	5299 Decker Rd, Holley, OH 72234
Wang	Amy	43 East Ave., Fairville, IN 80221

What field does not contain the smallest meaningful values?

address

Why would this be a data maintenance problem?

Not easy to query

What change to the table design should you make to correct this problem?

Separate into Street address, City, State, Zip

Remember, each field should hold the smallest meaningful value.

2.

LastName	FirstName	Project1	Time1	Project2	Time2
Abbott	Rob	AA-765	45%	QC-344	25%
Ballantyne	Carl	TS-1001	60%	AA-699	15%
Barefoot	Karen	QC-344	80%		
Sudore	Carrie	EN-29	20%	QC-405	65%
Wang	Amy	AA-780	30%		

What data normalization principle does this table violate?

Blank Spaces   Project # time #

Why would this be a data maintenance problem?

In the space below, enter the sample data as it would be displayed in a properly designed table.

1st name Last Name Project # % time

🖈 Remember, similar data belongs in the same field.

3.

	ProjectNumber	ProjectTitle	ProjectManager	Phone
	AA-699	Benefits Handbook	Atkinson	7472
	AA-765	Recognition Program	McMillan	7443
	AA-780	Appraisal Process	Atkinson	7472
	EN-29	Warehouse Rack System	Barnett	7387
	QC-344	Fulfillment Accuracy	Nguyen	7502
	QC-405	Customer Survey	Nguyen	7502
	TS-1001	New Product Testing	Cardinale	7311

What field contains unnecessarily repeated values?

Mgr Name + Phone # — what if Phone # changes

What data maintenance problem does this cause?

What tables would you need to eliminate the repeated values in the Phone field?

Separate table Proj Mgr Phone #   Proj Number
Proj Title
Proj Manager
Phone Field

Remember, repeated values in a field may mean there's too much information in the table and it should be broken into two or more tables.

4.

EmployeeId	LastName	FirstName	Address	City	State	Zip	Spouse
0027	McMillan	Lynne	270 Lima Rd.	Dustin	OH	72308	
0032	Wang	Amy	43 East Ave.	Fairville	IN	80221	
0042	Atkinson	Angela	1012 Main St.	Fairville	IN	80221	Jason
0049	Nguyen	Tram	45 Oak Dr.	Charter	IN	80219	Kia
0051	Sudore	Carrie	5299 Decker Rd.	Holley	OH	72234	John
0067	Barnett	Amy	4772 S. Union	Lyons	OH	72247	Kirk
0072	Barefoot	Karen	866 Colonial Dr.	Charter	IN	80219	
0078	Ballantyne	Carl	62 Crescent Ave.	Lyons	OH	72245	Melissa
0079	Cardinale	Alex	12 Cooper Dr., Apt. 2B	Holley	OH	72235	
0122	Abbott	Rob	107 6th St.	Holley	OH	72234	Jennifer

What field contains missing values?

Spouse

What data normalization principle does this violate?

What tables would eliminate the blank values?

Separate Field with Employee ID + Spouse

 Remember, a table with missing values may indicate that not all fields pertain to every record.

DISCOVERY ACTIVITY 2-6

Fixing Data Maintenance Problems

Scenario:

Now let's turn our attention to the draft tables for the computer inventory database and see if any of these potential data maintenance problems exist. You've decided that you need the following tables.

Employees
EmployeeName
Department

Computers
AssetTag
Manufacturer
Note
DateReceived
Warranty
PurchasePrice

Imagine that you've filled in the sample data shown in Figure 2-3 and Figure 2-4.

[Handwritten annotations surrounding the figures:]
- Employee table
- Break down First + Last name
- Assign #'s to depts
- Separate table for MFR + Code
- Create a Dept Code table
- Computer table Asset tag = MFR ID, Date Rec'd, Warranty purch
- Separate table for notes to include Asset tag

Employees : Table

EmployeeName	DeptName
Rob Abbott	Administration
Carl Ballantyne	Administration
Carrie Sudore	Fulfillment
Karen Barefoot	Sales
Amy Wang	Fulfillment

Figure 2-3: *The Employees table with sample data.*

Computers : Table

AssetTag	Manufacturer	DateReceived	PurchasePrice	Warranty	Note
1052	Cyber	10/19/2000	$1,250.00	☑	
1055	HiTech	9/7/1999	$2,700.00	☐	Laptop
1059	Micron	4/2/2000	$850.00	☐	
1066	HiTech	11/7/2000	$2,300.00	☑	Laptop
1072	Cyber	12/1/1999	$1,200.00	☐	
1073	Cyber	12/1/1999	$1,200.00	☐	
1075	Omni	6/30/2000	$1,500.00	☑	
1077	HiTech	2/28/2001	$1,050.00	☑	
1080	Omni	11/7/1999	$1,400.00	☐	
1093	HiTech	7/5/2000	$1,100.00	☑	
1124	Cyber	2/7/2001	$899.00	☑	
1164	Cyber	12/3/2000	$1,250.00	☑	
1168	Atlas	1/12/2001	$3,200.00	☑	Financial system server

Figure 2-4: *The Computers table with sample data.*

1. Examine the Employees table. In the space below, make notes on the changes you think should be made to the design of this table to meet the data normalization guidelines?

2. Now examine the Computers table. List below the changes that should be made to the design.

TOPIC F

Designate Primary and Foreign Keys

Now that you've modified the design of the tables so that you're confident that the data can be maintained accurately, it's time to work on the issue of primary and foreign key fields as the next step in your design procedure. Using key fields is an essential part of designing tables in a relational database.

Primary and foreign keys enable you to connect the data stored in different tables. They are also the way a relational database management system manages the integrity of your data.

Designate Primary Keys

Definition:

A *primary key* is a field or combination of fields that contains a value that uniquely identifies a record. Once you designate a field as a primary key, Access will require a value to be entered and will prevent any duplicate values from being entered in that field (so, for example, you won't inadvertently list the same employee twice). By default, Access sorts the records by the values in the primary key. The primary key is also used in establishing appropriate relationships between tables.

The characteristics to use in selecting a field or fields to serve as the primary key are that its values:

- Uniquely identify each record (no duplicate values).
- Are never blank.
- Rarely (if ever) change.
- Includes as few fields as possible.

Example:

Fields that are often used as primary key fields include:

- Employee ID number
- Student ID number
- Order number
- Item number
- Part number
- ISBN number
- Date plus time
- Serial number

Repeated Values in Foreign Key Fields

As you enter sample data in your tables, you may notice that, in some *foreign key* fields, there are repeated values. And then you might think "I thought tables weren't supposed to have repeated values in a field!" Database design principles say that it's okay to have repeated values in foreign key fields because, without them, you wouldn't be able to connect the data in different tables. The thinking is that the values in key fields rarely change, whereas the values in non-key fields are much more likely to be edited.

DISCOVERY ACTIVITY 2-7

Identifying Primary and Foreign Key Fields

Scenario:

Let's assume that our database design now contains the tables and fields shown in Figure 2-5. When you go to actually create the tables in Access, you'll need to designate a field or fields to be used as the primary key for each table. You also need to be sure you'll be able to connect related data, so we also need to check that we have all the foreign keys we need.

As you identify the key fields, mark the primary key field(s) with a P for each table in Figure 2-5. Foreign keys can be indicated with an F. If you find you need to add any key fields, add them to Figure 2-5 as well.

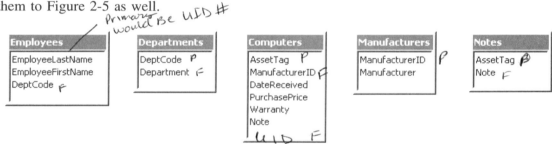

Figure 2-5: *Tables in the ComputerInventory database.*

1. What field or fields in the Employees table could serve as the primary key?

2. In the Departments table, what field could be the primary key?

3. What about the Computers table?

4. What would be the primary keys for the Manufacturers and the Notes tables?

_____

5. Now you need to make sure that you have the foreign keys necessary to connect related data held in separate tables. How will you relate the data in the Employees and Departments tables?

_____

6. How will you be able to relate a particular computer to a particular employee?

_____

7. What field will relate the data in the Manufacturers and Computers tables?

_____

8. How will you associate a Note with a particular computer?

_____

9. Compare your annotated figure (see Figure 2-6) to the one that follows.

Departments		Employees		Computers		Manufacturers		Notes
P DeptCode		LastName		P AssetTag		P ManufacturerID		P AssetTag
Department		FirstName		F ManufacturerID		Manufacturer		Note
		F DeptCode		DateReceived				
				PurchasePrice				
		P Employee ID		Warranty				
				F Employee ID				

Figure 2-6: *Primary and foreign keys in the ComputerInventory database.*

TOPIC G

Identify Table Relationships

You've done a lot of work on the design of your database and only one step remains in the process before you can begin actually building it in Access. All that remains is to identify the type of relationship that exists between the data in related tables.

When you implement your database design in Access, you will establish relationships between the tables. Access will "guess" at the type of relationship, but, to be sure that they're related correctly, you need to examine your sample data and know what the relationship should be.

Identify Table Relationships

There are two types of data relationships that can be implemented in Access 2002: a one-to-one relationship and a one-to-many relationship.

Guidelines

When reviewing the table relationships in your database, keep in mind:

- A one-to-one relationship means that each record in one table relates to a maximum of one record in another table.

- A one-to-many relationship means that each record in one table can potentially relate to more than one record in another table. Depending on which of the two tables you're looking at, you can also express this as a many-to-one relationship.

Example:

A common example of a one-to-one relationship is a table holding employee addresses and another table containing current employee pay rates. These might be contained in separate tables for security of the payroll data. A one-to-many relationship would be a table with customer information and another with customer order data.

In examining the relationships between data in tables, you may find that you have a many-to-many relationship between two tables. This is when many records in one table can relate to many records in another table. For example, if you had a table for employees and another for projects, you might find a many-to-many relationship if each employee could work on many projects and each project could involve many employees. This relationship cannot be implemented directly in Access and would have to be resolved by the creation of an intersection table containing, for example, just EmployeeID and ProjectNumber fields. This table would have a many-to-one relationship with both of the other tables.

Database Diagrams

When you're designing a database, it can be helpful to summarize the design by drawing a box for each table and listing the fields it will contain. This becomes your database diagram and it can be a very useful reference.

DISCOVERY ACTIVITY 2-8

Identifying Relationships

Scenario:

You're eager to set up your new computer inventory database. You just need to finalize your design diagram by indicating the type of relationship that exists between the data in related tables. This is also an opportunity to make sure that you don't have any unresolved many-to-many relationships because Access does not support them.

As you identify each relationship, use Figure 2-7 as your database diagram. Draw a line from the primary key field in one table to the foreign key field in each related table. Mark each end of the line with a 1 or an N, as appropriate, to indicate whether it is the one or the many side of the relationship. Primary key fields are in boldface in the diagram.

 Using N to indicate a many side of a relationship is a common technique used by database designers. In Access, you will see a many side of a relationship indicated by an infinity symbol (∞).

Figure 2-7: *The ComputerInventory database diagram.*

1.

DeptCode	Department
▶ 100	Administration
200	Finance
300	Fulfillment
400	Sales
500	Technical Services
*	

Departments : Table

Employees : Table

EmployeeID	LastName	FirstName	DeptCode
▶ 0026	Smith	Jason	300
0027	McMillan	Lynne	300
0032	Wang	Amy	300
0036	Brown	Andrea	200
0039	Kilinski	Susan	300
0042	Atkinson	Angela	400
0043	Coleman	William	100
0044	Tydings	Jennifer	400
0047	Sandler, Jr.	Todd	400
0048	Caldwell	Josh	300
0049	Nguyen	Tram	200
0051	Sudore	Carrie	300
0052	Moss	Greg	500

Examine the data in the Departments and Employees tables. What type of relationship exists between these tables?

How should you indicate this relationship in the database diagram?

2.

Manufacturers : Table

ManufacturerID	Manufacturer
▶ 1	HiTech
2	Omni
3	Micron
4	Cyber
5	Atlas

Computers : Table

AssetTag	ManufacturerID	DateReceived	PurchasePrice	Warranty	EmployeeID
▶ 1020	1	1/5/1999	$3,200.00	Yes	0075
1041	2	5/1/2000	$1,200.00	Yes	0057
1042	2	5/1/2000	$1,200.00	Yes	0063
1043	2	5/1/2000	$1,200.00	Yes	0067
1044	3	8/20/1999	$1,499.00	No	0056
1047	3	8/20/1999	$1,499.00	No	0047
1052	4	10/19/2000	$1,250.00	Yes	0036
1055	1	9/7/1999	$2,700.00	No	0044
1059	3	4/2/2000	$850.00	No	0053

What is the relationship between the Manufacturers and Computers tables?

3.

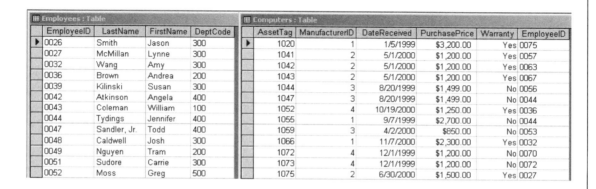

Now examine the data in the Computers and Notes tables. What is the relationship?

4.

The last set of related tables is Employees and Computers. What is that relationship?

5. Did your review of the relationships between the tables reveal any many-to-many relationships?

6.

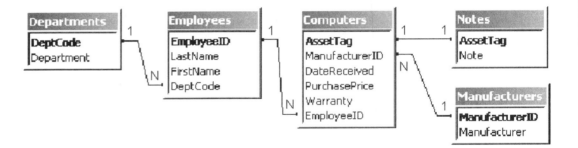

Does your completed diagram resemble the one above?

Lesson 2 Follow-up

Congratulations! You've covered all the steps required to plan an Access database. You began by identifying the database purpose. Next, you reviewed existing data, determined the fields you would include, and then grouped the fields into tables. After normalizing the data, you designated primary and foreign keys. Finally, you identified the relationships between tables, the last step before moving on to create your database.

1. **Why is it important to create a plan before building your database?**

2. **What fields might you include in the first database you need to build on your job? How would you group them into tables?**

LESSON 3
Building the Basic Structure

Lesson Time
45 minutes

Lesson Objectives:

In this lesson, you will create tables to hold data and then establish table relationships.

You will:

- Create a new blank database.
- Create a new table using a wizard.
- Relate the choices made in Design view to the display of data in Datasheet view.
- Create new tables in table Design view.
- Create relationships between tables.

Introduction

Once you've designed the database, you need to create the tables that will store the data. Although it is not required that you establish relationships between tables, it is certainly a good practice, as it is a mechanism for promoting data accuracy and it makes many aspects of working in Access easier. This lesson will introduce you to the basics of building tables and table relationships.

Since tables are the essential objects of all Access databases, any Access user will—at some time—want to create a table. Whether you're creating a whole new database or adding a table to an existing database to meet an expanded information need, the techniques are the same.

TOPIC A

Create a Blank Database

When you need a new database, your options are to create one based on a template from Microsoft, to base it on a copy of the structure of a database that you or someone else already has, or to create a blank database. The latter option enables you to totally customize the database to meet your needs and is usually the option of choice for implementing your database plan. That's the approach you'll take in this lesson.

Knowing how to create a new database of your very own design frees you from having to find an appropriate template or having to spend a lot of time modifying someone else's design.

Create a Blank Database

Procedure Reference: Create a New Blank Database

To create a new blank database:

1. Start Access.

2. If necessary, display the New File task pane by clicking on the New button.

3. In the New File task pane, under the New heading, click Blank Database.

4. Navigate to the location in which you wish to store the database file.

5. Assign a name to the database file.

6. Click Create.

ACTIVITY 3-1

Creating a New Blank Database

Scenario:

You've decided that you want a database that is precisely tailored to what you need to accomplish, so you want to start it from scratch. You will create and save a new Access MDB file, so you can then go on to create your own Access objects.

What You Do	How You Do It
1. Display the New File task pane and choose to create a Blank Database.	a. Click the New button or choose File→ New.
	b. In the New File task pane, under the New heading, **click on the Blank Database link.**
2. Name the new database *MyComputerInventory* and save it in the My Documents folder.	a. In the File Name text box, **type** *MyComputerInventory*.
	b. If necessary, in the Places bar, **click My Documents.**
	c. **Click Create.**

3. **Examine the Database window.** The name of the new database is displayed in the title bar. The title bar also indicates that the database is in Access 2000 file format.

TOPIC B

Create a Table using a Wizard

A new blank database is just that—blank. You also need to create all the appropriate tables to store your data. There is a wizard available to help you in creating tables so you'll try that out next. Wizards can simplify complex tasks for beginning users and can save work for all users.

There are wizards available to help you in creating Access objects. It's helpful to see what they are and how they work so you'll know when they might be useful to you.

Create a Table Using a Wizard

Procedure Reference: Create a New Table Using the Wizard

To create a new table using the wizard:

1. In the Database window, select Tables in the Objects bar.

2. Double-click on Create Table By Using Wizard.

3. Select the appropriate sample table.

4. From the sample table, add the sample fields you want to the new table.

5. If you wish, rename any fields by selecting the field and clicking Rename Field. Enter the new name and click OK.

6. Click Next.

7. Assign a name to your table and select whether you want the wizard to set the primary key or whether you wish to select it yourself.

8. Click Next.

9. If you choose to set the primary key yourself:
    a. Select the field that contains a unique value for each record.
    b. Indicate the type of data you want the primary key field to contain.
    c. Click Next.

10. If there are already other tables in your database:
    a. Indicate whether the new table is related to any of them.
    b. If the new table is related to an existing table, select that table, click Relationships, and select the type of relationship.
    c. Click OK.
    d. Click Next.

11. Select whether you want, after the table is created, to modify the design, enter data directly in the table, or have the wizard create and display a form for you to use to enter data. Click Finish.

Let Access Set the Primary Key

If you choose to let the wizard set the primary key for you, one of two things will happen. If you included an ID field in your new table, Access will designate that as the primary key and will make it an AutoNumber data type. This means that Access will enter unique sequential numbers in that field as you enter records. If there is not an ID field in your table, the wizard will add one with the same name as the table followed by the abbreviation ID. This field will be designated as an AutoNumber data type. You cannot change the values entered by Access in an AutoNumber field.

When are Numbers not Numbers?

Even though a field, such as an EmployeeID field, may contain numbers, it should not necessarily be considered to contain numbers for working in Access. Examples of this are phone numbers and Social Security numbers. You should only consider the field to contain numbers if you will need to perform mathematical operations on the data.

ACTIVITY 3-2

Create a Table with a Wizard

Scenario:

You're creating your new database and want to start building the tables you need as quickly as possible, so you've decided to try using a wizard. From your database diagram shown in Figure 3-1, you've decided to create the table for information on employees first. Assume that the employees have IDs assigned by the company.

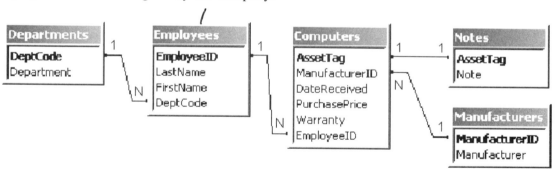

Figure 3-1: *Diagram for the MyComputerInventory database.*

What You Do	How You Do It
1. Start the Table Wizard.	a. If necessary, in the Objects bar, **select Tables.**
	b. **Double-click on Create Table By Using Wizard.**

2. Review the list of Business and Personal sample tables that are available.

    a. With Business selected, **scroll the Sample Tables list** to see what tables are available.

    b. **Select Personal.**

    c. **Scroll the Sample Tables list.**

3. Using the Business sample tables, **create an Employees table including the EmployeeID, FirstName, and LastName fields.**

    a. **Select Business.**

    b. In the list of Sample tables, **select Employees.**

    c. In the Sample Fields list, **select EmployeeID.**

    d. **Click on the right pointing arrow**   `>` .

    e. In the Sample Fields list, **select FirstName.**

    f. **Click on the right pointing arrow.**

    g. In the Sample Fields list, **select LastName.**

    h. **Click on the right pointing arrow.**

4. The database diagram calls for a DeptCode field. The closest one in the Sample Fields list is DepartmentName. **Add the DepartmentName field to the table, rename it *DeptCode*, and then continue with the wizard.**

    a. In the Sample Fields list, **select DepartmentName.**

    b. **Click on the right pointing arrow.**

    c. **Click Rename Field.**

    d. In the Rename Field text box, **type *DeptCode*.**

    e. **Click OK.**

    f. **Click Next.**

5. Notice that the table will be named Employees, which is just what your diagram calls for. The wizard explains about a primary key and asks if you want the wizard to set it or if you want to set it yourself. Since you know that you need to be able to enter the IDs assigned by the company, **choose to set the primary key yourself and continue with the wizard.**

  a. **Select No, I'll Set The Primary Key.**

  b. **Click Next.**

6. Notice that the wizard assumes that you want to use the EmployeeID field which matches your plan. Since you won't be performing mathematical operations on the IDs, **specify that you want the data to be numbers and/or letters that you'll be entering. Continue with the wizard.**

  a. **Accept the default field entry of EmployeeID.**

  b. **Select Numbers And/Or Letters I Enter When I Add New Records.**

  c. **Click Next.**

7. You could have the wizard create a simple form to use for data entry, but you'll work on forms later. **Choose to enter data directly in the table and complete with the wizard.**

  a. **Select Enter Data Directly Into The Table.**

  b. **Click Finish.**

TOPIC C

Compare Datasheet and Design Views

All Access objects have two faces—the view you see of tables, forms, and so on, when they display data, and a view where you make the choices that determine how the object will look and function. This topic will introduce the elements of that second view.

Even if you never have to build a table from scratch, you may still need to change something about the design of a table. For example, you may be working with a table created by someone else who is no longer with the company and the need for data has changed.

The Table Design Environment

The table's Design window contains two panes (refer to Figure 3-2). In the upper pane, you designate the fields you want in the table and assign the appropriate data type. You can also enter a description of the field. The lower pane is the Field Properties pane. For the field selected in the upper pane, the Field Properties pane displays the appropriate properties that you can set for the field. The right side of the Field Properties pane displays explanations relevant to whatever you have selected in either pane.

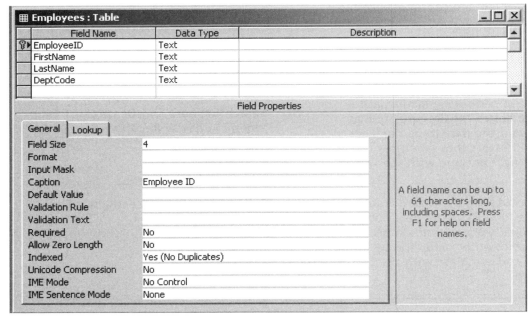

Figure 3-2: *An example of a table's Design view.*

Compare Datasheet and Design Views

The column headings and format of the data that you see in Datasheet view are determined by the entries and selections you make in Design view.

Caption Property

By default, the name of the field is used as the column heading in Datasheet view. If you wish to display a heading different from the field name, select the field in Design view and enter the heading in the Caption property box. For example, if you are following the convention of not having spaces in your field names, you could enter a caption that includes spaces.

Text Data Type

Text is the default data type. A Text field can contain letters, numbers that don't require calculations, or a combination of letters and numbers. It can contain up to 255 characters.

Activity 3-3

Comparing Datasheet and Design Views

Setup:
The Employees table is open in Datasheet view.

Scenario:
Now that you've created your first table, you want to familiarize yourself with how it looks in Datasheet view. You also want to see the design that the wizard created for you.

What You Do	How You Do It
1. Notice that each field is displayed as a column in the datasheet. **What difference do you notice in the column headings?**	
2. **Change to Design view.**	a. **Click Design View** 📐 .
3. **Examine the Field Name column.** The field names do not have spaces in them.	
4. **Now look at the Field Properties pane.** The properties for the field selected in the field list are displayed. The Caption property for the EmployeeID field is set to Employee ID—which has a space and is displayed as the column heading.	
5. **Examine the Data Type column.** The wizard assumed that the FirstName, LastName, and DeptCode fields will contain text. Because you indicated that the EmployeeID field could contain numbers and/or letters, it is also a Text data type.	
6. **Notice the Field Size box in the lower portion of the window.** The EmployeeID field was assigned a size of 4 by the wizard.	
7. **Select the FirstName field and note the field size.**	a. **Click on the record selector to the left of the FirstName field.** The Field Size is set to 50. This is the default value for a Text field.
8. **Notice the small key icon** 🔑 **to the left of the EmployeeID field.** This shows that you selected this field to be the primary key for this table.	
9. **Close the Employees: Table window.**	a. **Click the Close button.**
10. Notice that the Employees table is displayed in the Database window.	

TOPIC D

Create Tables in Design View

You've created a table with the Table Wizard and have acquainted yourself with the table's design environment. Now you'll create some additional tables by working in Design view, rather than by using the wizard.

There may not always be an appropriate sample table available in the Table Wizard, so it's good to know how to create a new table on your own.

Access Data Types

When you're creating a table and deciding on data types for each field, you need to know what kind of data the field will contain in order to make an appropriate choice of a data type. Table 3-1 explains the different kinds of data types available.

 As you decide on the data types for your fields, it's a good idea to make note of them on your database diagram.

Table 3-1: *The Access Data Types*

Data Type	Description
Text	Letters, numbers that don't require calculations, or combinations of letters and numbers. Can contain up to 255 characters.
Memo	Lengthy text. Can contain up to 65,535 characters.
Number	Numbers to be used in mathematical calculations.
Date/Time	Date and time values.
Currency	Currency values and other numeric data requiring high precision in calculations.
AutoNumber	Unique values assigned by Access.
Yes/No	Yes/No, True/False, or On/Off values.
OLE Object	An object, such as a graphic or a Word or Excel document.
Hyperlink	A hyperlink address of a Web site or a file.
Lookup Wizard	Allows you to choose a value from a table of a list of values that you enter.

Create Tables in Design View

Procedure Reference: Create a New Table in Design View

To create a new table in Design view:

1. In the Database window, in the Objects bar, select Tables.

2. Double-click on Create Table In Design View.

3. For each field you wish to include in the table:

   a. In the Field Name column, enter the name of the field.

   b. Click in the Data Type column for the field, display the drop-down list, and select the data type.

    c.   Make any changes you want to the Field Properties displayed in the lower pane.

    4.   Select the field(s) you want to set as the primary key and click the Primary Key button.

    5.   Click the Save button.

    6.   Enter a name for the table.

    7.   Click OK.

Field Size Property

The Field Size property is available for Text, Number, and AutoNumber fields. Your database will perform more efficiently and will occupy less storage space if you set the Field Size property to conform with the actual length of the data you will store in the field. Look in Access Help for the topic on the FieldSize Property for details on the various settings.

An AutoNumber Field as a Foreign Key

When you have an AutoNumber field as the primary key in one table and wish to use that same field as a foreign key in another table, in that second table, you must set the field's data type to Number and the Field Size property to Long Integer.

ACTIVITY 3-4

Creating and Saving a Table

Setup:

The MyComputerInventory database is open.

Scenario:

You're continuing on implementing the design of your computer inventory database (shown in Figure 3-1). Since there aren't appropriate sample tables available for all the tables you need, you're going to create the rest in Design view.

What You Do	How You Do It
1. Let's create the Manufacturers table first. **Open a table Design window for a new table.**	a. **Double-click on Create Table In Design View.**
2. **Enter *ManufacturerID* as the first field name.**	a. In the first field in the Field Name column, **type *ManufacturerID*.**

3. For every field, you must select a data type. Since there aren't assigned IDs for various manufacturers, you will let Access assign them a unique number. **Set the data type to AutoNumber.**

   a. **Click in the Data Type field for the ManufacturerID record.**

   b. **Click on the down arrow** to open the Data Type drop-down list.

   c. **Select AutoNumber.**

---

4. **Notice that an AutoNumber field has a Field Size of Long Integer.**

---

5. **Enter the** *Manufacturer* **field with a data type of Text and a Field Size of** *30*.

   a. **Click in the second field in the Field Name column.**

   b. **Type** *Manufacturer*.

   c. **Press [Tab].** The Text data type is the default.

   d. In the Field Properties pane, **select the value in the Field Size property box.**

   e. **Type** *30*.

---

6. **Set the ManufacturerID field as the primary key.**

   a. **Click on the record selector** to select the ManufacturerID record.

   b. On the toolbar, **click the Primary Key button.**

---

7. **Save the table with the name** *Manufacturers* **and close the Design window.**

   a. **Click Save.**

   b. In the Table Name text box, **type** *Manufacturers*.

   c. **Click OK.**

   d. **Click Close.**

 If you notice in the Database window that you misspelled the name of the table, you can change it. Right-click on the table name and choose Rename. Enter the correct name and press [Enter].

ACTIVITY 3-5

Create Another Table

Scenario:

Now that you've successfully created your first table in Design view, you're ready to create the one to hold information on computers. You can refer to your database diagram in Figure 3-1 for the fields you need and how this table is going to relate to others in the database.

What You Do	How You Do It
1. Open a new table Design window and enter *AssetTag* as the first field with a data type of Text and a field size of *4*.	a. Double-click on Create Table In Design View.
	b. Type *AssetTag*.
	c. Press [Tab].
	d. Select the value in the Field Size property box.
	e. Type *4*.

2. **Refer to the database diagram.** The next field is ManufacturerID. It is a foreign key to the primary key in the Manufacturers table. Because you specified that field as an AutoNumber field, the foreign key field must have a Number data type with a field size of Long Integer.

3. Enter the *ManufacturerID* field with a data type of Number and a Field Size property of Long Integer.	a. In the next Field Name field, **type** *ManufacturerID*.
	b. Open the Data Type drop-down list and select Number.
	c. Verify that the Field Size property is set to Long Integer.
4. Enter the *DateReceived* field with a Date/Time data type. Set the display of dates to the format 9/15/ 2001.	a. In the next Field Name field, **type** *DateReceived*.
	b. Open the Data Type drop-down list and select Date/Time.
	c. Click in the Format property box.
	d. Open the Format drop-down list and select Short Date.

LESSON 3

5. Enter the *PurchasePrice* field with a Currency data type to be displayed with no decimal places.	a. In the next Field Name field, **type** *PurchasePrice*.
	b. **Open the Data Type drop-down list and select Currency.**
	c. **Open the Decimal Places property drop-down list and select 0.**
6. Enter the *Warranty* field as a Yes/No data type.	a. In the next Field Name field, **type** *Warranty*.
	b. **Open the Data Type drop-down list and select Yes/No.**
7. Enter the *EmployeeID* field as a Text data type with a field size of *4*.	a. In the next Field Name field, **type** *EmployeeID*.
	b. **Open the Data Type drop-down list and select Text.**
	c. **Select the value in the Field Size property box and type *4*.** EmployeeID is a foreign key to the Employees table and the primary key of that table has a field size of 4.
8. Set the primary key to AssetTag.	a. **Select the AssetTag field.**
	b. **Click Primary Key.**
9. Save the table as *Computers* and close the table Design window.	a. **Click Save.**
	b. In the Table Name text box, **type** *Computers*.
	c. **Click OK.**
	d. **Click Close.**

PRACTICE ACTIVITY 3-6

Completing the Tables for the Database

Scenario:

You need just two more tables to finish the implementation of your database design. You have your database diagram in Figure 3-1, your notes about data types, and the previous activities as resources.

1. **Create and save the Departments table with the following specifications:**
   - A DeptCode field with a data type of Text and a field size of 3.
   - A Department field with a data type of Text and a field size of 50.
   - The DeptCode field as the primary key.

2. **Create and save the Notes table with the following specifications:**
   - An AssetTag field with a data type of Text and a field size of 4.
   - A Note field with a data type of Memo.
   - The AssetTag field as the primary key.

TOPIC E

Create Relationships between Tables

Once you've built the tables you need in your database, the last step in implementing your design is to establish the appropriate relationships between the tables. You also need to think about enforcing referential integrity in your database.

You can't harness the full power of a relational database management system like Access without establishing table relationships and using referential integrity. Together, these features make your work and data maintenance more efficient and help promote the accuracy of the data.

Referential Integrity

Referential integrity ensures that you don't accidently delete or change data that would invalidate the relationship between tables.

Guidelines

You can set referential integrity between two tables if the following are true:
- The matching field is a primary key in one table or has a unique index.
- The related fields have the same data type (the exception is that an AutoNumber field can be related to a Number data type with a field size of Long Integer).

- Both tables are in the same Access database.

Example:

When referential integrity is enforced, certain rules apply to the data. The following list gives you some examples.

- You can't enter a value in the foreign key field of one table if there is not a matching value in the primary key of the related table.

- You can't delete a record from the primary table (the table in which the primary key is the related field) if a matching record exists in the related table.

- You can't change the value in the primary key of the primary table if there are related records in the related table.

Create Relationships between Tables

Procedure Reference: Create a Relationship and Enforce Referential Integrity

To create a relationship between two tables and enforce referential integrity between them:

1. Choose Tools→Relationships to open the Relationships window.

2. In the Show Table dialog box, select the tables you want to work with and click Add.

    🖈 To select multiple tables in the Show Table dialog box, you can use [Shift]-click to select contiguous tables and [Ctrl]-click to select non-contiguous tables.

3. Close the Show Table dialog box.

4. Select the primary key field in one table that you want to relate to the foreign key field in the second table.

5. Drag the primary key to the foreign key.

6. In the Edit Relationships dialog box, check Enforce Referential Integrity.

7. Click Create.

8. Close the Relationships window, saving changes to its layout.

ACTIVITY 3-7

Create Relationships between Tables

Setup:

The MyComputerInventory database is open and the Employees, Manufacturers, Computers, Departments, and Notes tables have been created.

Scenario:

By analyzing some sample data, you've already determined what types of relationships there are between your tables, so you're ready to finish up the implementation of the design of your database by creating those relationships. You want to help ensure the accuracy of the data, so you've decided to enforce referential integrity in all relationships. You do this by working in the Relationships window.

What You Do	How You Do It
1. Open the Relationships window, add all five tables to the window, and close the Show Table dialog box.	a. Choose Tools→Relationships.
	b. With Computers selected on the Tables tab of the Show Table dialog box, **press [Shift], and select Notes** in the list of tables.
	c. **Click Add.**
	d. **Click Close.**
2. Adjust the size of the Computers table so you can view the entire list of fields.	a. Place the mouse pointer over the bottom edge of the Computers table until the mouse pointer becomes a vertical double-headed arrow.
	b. Drag the bottom border down until you can view all fields and the vertical scroll bar is no longer displayed.
3. **Notice the order of the tables in the window.** They are displayed in alphabetical order. It will be easier to drag to create relationships if the tables with related data are next to each other.	

4. **Rearrange the tables so they are displayed in the order below.**

    a. **Point to the title bar of a table you wish to move.**

    b. **Drag the table to the desired location.**

5. You've already determined that there is a one-to-many relationship between the Departments and Employees tables. **Create the relationship.**

    a. In the Departments table, **select the DeptCode field.**

    b. **Drag the DeptCode field of the Departments table to the DeptCode field in the Employees table.**

6. In the Edit Relationships dialog box, **notice the Relationship Type.** Because you dragged the primary key from one table to a foreign key in another table, Access assumed there is a one-to-many relationship.

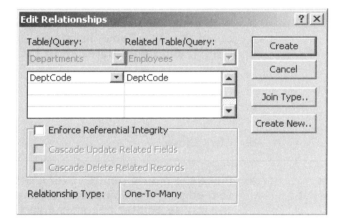

7. **Enforce referential integrity in this relationship.**

    a. In the Edit Relationships dialog box, **check Enforce Referential Integrity.**

    b. **Click Create.**

8. Now create the one-to-one relationship between the Computers and Notes tables and enforce referential integrity in the relationship.

a. Drag the AssetTag field from either the Computers or Notes table to the AssetTag field in the other table.

 When creating a one-to-one relationship, it doesn't matter which primary key field you select.

b. Verify that the Relationship Type is One-To-One.

c. Check Enforce Referential Integrity.

d. Click Create.

PRACTICE ACTIVITY 3-8

Completing the Relationships

Referential integrity

Scenario:

You've successfully established two table relationships, so now you can complete the implementation of your design by creating the remaining relationships.

1. Using Figure 3-1 as a guide, **establish the appropriate relationships between the remaining tables enforcing referential integrity between them.**

 When you go to create the relationship between the Manufacturers and Computers tables, be sure to drag the primary key (the ManufacturerID field in the Manufacturers table) to the foreign key (the ManufacturerID field in the Computers table).

2. **Check your results against Figure 3-3.**

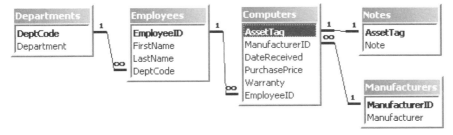

Figure 3-3: *The relationships in the MyComputerInventory database.*

3. **Close the Relationships window being sure to save the changes to the layout.**

 Be sure to save the changes to the layout of the Relationships window or the graphical representation of the relationships will not be displayed the next time you open the window.

4. **Close the MyComputerInventory database.**

5. In the Database window, **click the Close button or choose File→Close.**

Lesson 3 Follow-up

Creating a blank database is fairly easy, but adding custom tables can be a little trickier. When time is of the essence, you can build tables on the fly with the Table Wizard. If customization is key, you'll need to build your tables in Design view. Once you have your tables in place, creating the right relationships between them is the next step toward harnessing the power of your data.

1. **In what circumstances would you prefer to create a database using a template over creating one from scratch?**

2. **Do you think the Table Wizard will offer most of the table-building functions you require, or will you often build tables in Datasheet view?**

LESSON 4
Working with Tables

Lesson Objectives:

In this lesson, you will modify the design of and work with data in tables.

You will:

• Modify the design of a table to better display the data it holds.

• Work in a table's datasheet view to find and edit records.

• Use a subdatasheet to view related records.

Introduction

Creating tables is only the first step in building the core of your database. You also need to know how to make changes to the design of tables and to work with the data you store in them.

It's rare to get the design of a table exactly right on the first try, so you need to know how to make improvements. Also, your information needs may change over time or you may inherit a database from someone else. And a table isn't much use if you don't know how to work with the data it holds.

TOPIC A

Modify a Table Design

Despite your best efforts to anticipate your needs for fields in a table, sometimes it isn't until you actually start entering records that you realize the design of a table could use some improvement. Or you may inherit a table from someone else and want to change some of the choices that person made. In this topic, you'll see how to make changes that improve the display and usability of the data.

You'll want your tables to be as user-friendly as possible and to appropriately display the data stored in the fields. To do this, you need to know the effects of various choices and field properties.

Modify a Table Design

Procedure Reference: Modify the Design of a Table

To modify the design of a table:

1. Open the table in Design view.

2. Add a field.

   a. To add a field, click in a blank Field Name row or click on the record selector for the field below where you want the new field and choose Insert→ Rows.

   b. Enter the field name and choose the appropriate entry in the Data Type column.

   c. If necessary, change or set field properties.

3. To delete a field, click on the record selector for the field and press [Delete].

4. To change or set properties for a field, click the field name and make the entries in the Field Properties pane.

5. To change a data type, open the Data Type drop-down list for the field and select the new data type.

Entering a New Record

In an Access table, new records are always entered in the record at the end of the table that displays an asterisk (*). After you enter the data and move off the record, it is saved in the table in order by the primary key.

Saving Data

New or edited data in a record is saved when you move the focus off the record, choose Records→Save Record, or press [Shift][Enter]. A pencil icon is displayed on the record selector, as you enter or edit data, and is not displayed once the data has been saved.

ACTIVITY 4-1

Modifying the Design of a Table

Data Files:

- SampleTables.mdb

Scenario:

To illustrate techniques for working with tables, we need to use tables with specific kinds of data. So, for the moment, imagine that you've taken a new position in Human Resources and now have to use a database that had just been created by your predecessor. Before you do a lot of data entry, you want to take a look to see if you think the design is okay. You'll try the table out by entering a new record.

The record you're going to enter will contain the following data values:

- ID: 0023
- LN: Carney
- Dept: MK
- Health: Yes
- HD: today's date
- Hours: 37.5
- PayRate: 21.00

What You Do	How You Do It
1. From the My Documents folder, **open the SamplesTables database and open the Personnel table in Datasheet view.**	a. **Click Open.**
	b. If necessary, in the Places bar, **click My Documents.**
	c. In the list of files, **double-click on SampleTables.**
	d. In the list of tables in the Database window, **double-click on Personnel.**

LESSON 4

2. **Observe the datasheet.** The current record is indicated by the triangle icon on the record selector. A new record is indicated by the asterisk (*) on the record selector.

3. **Enter the new record, noting changes to the icon on the record selector as you work. (Use the data values mentioned in the scenario.) Save the record when you're done.**

   a. **Click in the ID field for the new record.** Notice that the asterisk (*) changes to a triangle.

   b. **Type *0023*.** The triangle changes to a pencil icon as soon as you begin to type.

   c. **Press [Enter] or [Tab]** to move to the next field.

   d. **Type *Carney*. Press [Enter].**

   e. **Type *MK* and press [Enter].**

   f. **Click in the checkbox or press [Spacebar]** to indicate a value of Yes. **Press [Enter].**   *Control*)

   g. **Type** today's date and **press [Enter].**

   🖈 You can enter the current date from your computer's system clock by pressing [Ctrl];.

   h. **Type *37.5* and press [Enter].**

   i. **Type *21.00*.**

   j. **Press [Enter] or click on another record** to save the new record. Notice that the pencil icon is no longer displayed.

4. **Observe the data.** The Hd column heading could be more descriptive. There are now two records with a last name of Carney, so a first name field would be helpful. The value you entered in the Hours field was rounded. The values in the Pay Rate field are displayed without decimals; it would be good to have them displayed as currency.

   Imagine also that you would like to view the ID field at the right of the datasheet and that you've been told you don't need to track enrollment in the health plan in this database after all. So you'll make these changes.

5.	Change to Design view and insert a *FirstName* field after the LastName field. Set Field Size to *20*.	a. Click Design View.
		b. Click on the record selector for the field below where you want to insert a field (Dept, in this case).
		c. Right-click on the selected record and choose Insert Rows.
		d. Type *FirstName*.
		e. Select the value in the Field Size property box and type *20*.
6.	For the HD field to have a column heading that is more descriptive, you can either change the field name or set a Caption for the field. **Use the latter technique so the column heading will be *HireDate*.**	a. In the upper pane, **select the HD field.**
		b. Click in the Caption property box.
		c. Type *HireDate*.
7.	Change the appropriate properties for the Hours field, so it will display one decimal place.	a. Select the Hours field.
		b. Open the Field Size drop-down list and select Double.
		c. Open the Format property drop-down list and select Fixed.
		d. Open the Decimal drop-down list and select 1.
8.	Change the PayRate field to a Currency data type with the appropriate display Format.	a. Select the PayRate field.
		b. Open the Data Type drop-down list and select Currency.
		c. Open the Format property drop-down list and select Currency.
9.	Delete the Health field and the data it contains, and then save the changes to the table design.	a. Click on the record selector to select the Health field.
		b. Press [Delete].
		c. Click Yes.
		d. Click Save.

10. **Change to Datasheet view and observe the effects of the changes to the table design.**

   a. Click Datasheet view.

   b. Observe the HireDate column heading.

   c. Note that the FirstName field is displayed in the order you entered it in Design view.

   d. Note that the Hours field includes one decimal place.

   e. Note that the values in the PayRate field are displayed as currency.

   f. Note that the Health field has been deleted.

11. **If you want to view the ID as the right-most column, you could move its position in the design of the table. Or you can leave it where it is in the table structure and just change it in the datasheet. Select the ID column and move it after the PayRate column.**

   a. Place the mouse pointer over the ID column heading until it becomes a downward-pointing arrow.

   b. **Click on the column heading** to select the column.

   c. Point to the column heading and drag it to the right until a dark line appears at the right edge of the PayRate column.

   d. Release the mouse button.

12. **Close the datasheet window, saving changes to the layout.**

   a. Click Close.

   b. Click Yes.

TOPIC B

Work in Datasheet View

Tables can be very large containing more fields than can be viewed on a screen and many thousands of records. This topic will show you some techniques for viewing, finding, and editing values in a datasheet.

An Access table can contain up to 255 fields and the number of records can occupy almost 2 GB (that's 2 billion bytes) of computer storage space. Normally, your tables will be nowhere near that big, but you'll still want to know how to efficiently view, find, and edit the record you need.

Work in Datasheet View

When you view records in a datasheet, Access provides a navigation bar in the bottom-left corner of the datasheet, as seen in Figure 4-1. You can use this navigation bar to move to various records. In addition, there are a number of mouse and keyboard techniques you can use to view different sets of records; they are summarized in Table 4-1.

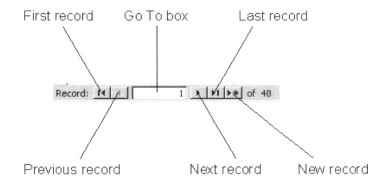

Figure 4-1: *The navigation bar.*

Table 4-1: *Mouse and Keyboard Navigation Techniques*

Tool	Navigation Technique	How it Works
Mouse	scroll bar arrows	Click to move the view one field or record at a time.
	scroll box	Drag to view the records you want.
	click in scroll bar	Click next to the scroll box to move a screenful at a time.
Keyboard	[Page Down], [Page Up]	Moves the view a screenful of records at a time.
	[Ctrl][Page Down], [Ctrl][Page Up]	Moves the view a screenful of fields at a time.

ACTIVITY 4-2

Working in Datasheet View

Setup:
The SampleTables database is open.

Scenario:
Among the tables you need to work with is one that's quite large and not all the fields and records can be viewed on your computer screen. You want to familiarize yourself with the data, and then you have a couple of edits you need to make.

What You Do	How You Do It
1. **Open the Employees table and use the horizontal and vertical scroll bars** to view all of the fields and all of the records.	a. Using the horizontal scroll bar, **click on the right arrow until you can view the rest of the fields.**
	b. Using the horizontal scroll bar, **drag the scroll box to the left until you can view the EmployeeID field.**
	c. Using the vertical scroll bar, **click on the down arrow until you can view the last record.**
	d. Using the vertical scroll bar, **drag the scroll box up until you can view the first record (the record for Jason Smith).**
2. Some people prefer to use keyboard shortcuts, so let's try some of those. **Use the [Page Down] and [Page Up] keys to view records, and then try them in combination with the [Ctrl] key to view fields.**	a. **Press [Page Down]** to view the next screen of records.
	b. **Press [Page Up]** to view the previous screen.
	c. **Press [Ctrl][Page Down]** to view the next screen of fields.
	d. **Press [Ctrl][Page Up]** to view the previous screen of fields.

3. As shown in Figure 4-1, Access provides a navigation bar in the lower-left corner of the screen. **Use the Last Record and First Record navigation buttons** to view the records.

   a. **Click the Last Record navigation button** . This positions the last record at the bottom of the window and makes it the current record.

   b. **Click the First Record navigation button** . This positions the first record at the top of the window and makes it the current record.

---

4. When all the fields don't fit on the screen, you can lose track of what record you're viewing when you scroll to view more fields. **Freeze the EmployeeID, LastName, and FirstName columns, and then scroll to view the Title field next to the names. Unfreeze the columns when you're done.**

   a. **Place the mouse pointer over the EmployeeID column heading until it becomes a downward-pointing arrow.**

   b. **Click on the column heading and drag to also select the LastName and FirstName columns.**

   c. **Choose Format→Freeze Columns.**

   d. **Click away from the selected column** to deselect it.

   e. **Use the horizontal scroll bar to view the Title field next to the names.**

   f. **Choose Format→Unfreeze All Columns.**

---

5. When a table is created, all the columns are the same standard width. For some fields, that may be wider than necessary and, for others, it's too narrow to view the data. **Drag the right edge of the Address column heading to the right so you can view the data.**

   Now double-click on the right edge of the State column heading to size it to fit the data.

   🖉 You can also size a column to fit the data by clicking in any field in the column, choosing Format→Column Width, and then clicking Best Fit.

   a. **Place the mouse pointer over the right edge of the Address column heading until it becomes a vertical bar with a double-headed horizontal arrow.**

   b. **Drag the column heading to the right.**

   c. **Place the mouse pointer over the right edge of the State column heading until it becomes a vertical bar with a double-headed horizontal arrow.**

   d. **Double-click on the right edge of the State column heading.**

---

6. You may want to view the records in an order other than by the primary key. **Sort the records by last name.**

   a. **Click on the LastName column heading.**

   b. **Click the Sort Ascending button** .

---

7. You'll often want to find a particular record and don't want to have to scroll through many records and fields to do so. Say that an employee, Michelle Rivera, has changed her name to Rivera-Lopez and you need to edit her record. On the toolbar, **use the Find button to locate her record.**

   a. **Click in any record in the LastName column.**

   b. **Click the Find button** .

   c. In the Find What text box, **type Rivera.** Notice that because you clicked in the LastName column, LastName is entered in the Look In box. By default, the value you typed must match the entry in the whole field so, for example, Riverati would not be found.

   d. **Click Find Next.**

   e. **When the record is found, click Cancel.**

8. **Change to Edit mode, add -Lopez to the existing value, and save the revised record.**

   a. **Press [F2].**

   b. **Type -Lopez.**

   c. **Press the up or down arrow** to move off the record and save it.

9. **Close the datasheet window, being sure to save changes to the layout.**

   a. **Close Close.**

   b. **Click Yes.**

TOPIC C

Work with Subdatasheets

Another reason for establishing relationships between your tables is that it enables the use of subdatasheets. They are a quick and easy way to view related records.

Imagine that you have tables containing thousands of records. The more data you have to manage, the more important it becomes to find ways to work with it efficiently. Subdatasheets can help you do that.

Work with Subdatasheets

When you establish table relationships in the Relationships window, subdatasheets are automatically displayed. By default, the subdatasheet displays records from the table that has a many-to-one relationship with the table open in Datasheet view.

- To expand a subdatasheet and view the related records, click the expand indicator (+).

- To collapse a subdatasheet, click the collapse indicator (-).
- To remove a subdatasheet from Datasheet view, choose Format→Subdatasheet→Remove.
- To change which related table is displayed as a subdatasheet, choose Insert→ Subdatasheet, select the table you wish to view, and click OK.

ACTIVITY 4-3

Working with Subdatasheets

Scenario:

Imagine that you're responsible for managing your company's records about customers and orders. You get a lot of questions about this information and need a quick way to provide answers. You decide to see how subdatasheets might help you. The database you're using has the tables and relationships shown in Figure 4-2.

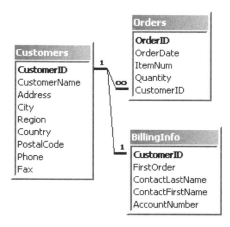

Figure 4-2: *Tables about customers, orders, and billing information.*

What You Do	How You Do It
1. **Open the Customers table.** You know there's a subdatasheet available because of the expand indicator ⊞ to the left of the first field. **Open the subdatasheet for the first record.**	a. With the list of tables displayed in the Database window, **double-click on Customers.** b. **Click the expand indicator** ⊞ to the left of the first record.
2. **Observe the subdatasheet.** It displays the related records from the Orders table. It's a quick way to check the orders for a particular customer.	
3. **Close the subdatasheet, and then view the subdatasheet for some of the other records.**	a. **Click the collapse indicator** ⊟. b. **Click the expand indicator for the record for which you wish to view related records.**

4. Say you decide you would like to view the related records from the BillingInfo table instead of the Orders data. **Use the Insert menu to change the subdatasheet.**

   a. **Choose Insert→Subdatasheet.**

   b. On the Tables tab of the Insert Subdatasheet dialog box, **select BillingInfo.**

   c. **Click OK.**

5. **Verify that the BillingInfo subdatasheet is now available, and then close the Customers window without saving changes to the layout.**

   a. **Click the expand indicator for a record.**

   b. **Click Close.**

   c. **Click No.**

Lesson 4 Follow-up

Tables are the basic building blocks of databases, and as you have seen, you can use them in many ways. You may wish to modify the design of tables in a database that you have inherited from someone else, or you may want to go back and tweak a table that you created with the Table Wizard. Your need to make adjustments won't end once you've customized the tables to your satisfaction. You're bound to have a need to view, find, and edit data values stored in your tables. Now that your tables are in good order, you're ready to begin creating and working with queries.

1. **When might you find the need to modify a table's design?**

2. **Which methods for viewing and finding information in Datasheet view do you think you will use most often? Why?**

LESSON 5

Creating and Working with Select Queries

Lesson Objectives:

In this lesson, you will create, modify the design of, and work with select queries.

You will:

- Relate the design of a select query to the contents of the datasheet.
- Create a select query using a wizard.
- Create select queries in query Design view.
- Use various criteria in queries to select records.
- Edit values in a query datasheet.
- Create a calculated field in a query using the Expression Builder.
- Create a summary calculation for a group of records.

Introduction

Your data is actually stored in tables, but select queries are the most frequently used means of selecting, sorting, and combining data from tables for everyday use. They are often the basis for forms and reports.

Sometimes you'll create a select query and use it over and over to produce the data for a report or a data entry form; you may even have some queries already that someone else created for you. There will also be times when you need to answer an unanticipated question about your data and you'll need to know how to create a select query in order to answer it.

 Please note that the data examples in this course are intentionally small for ease of use in class. Your own tables are likely to contain many more records.

TOPIC A

Examine a Query

In the brief tour of a database, you were able to see an example of a query. In this topic, you discuss how a query works and what you use it for.

Also, as with all Access objects, the design of the object determines the display of the data. The query design environment is unique, so you'll have an opportunity to familiarize yourself with it and see how it drives the display of the query datasheet.

Every database person should know what the purposes of queries are and how to use them. This is your chance to add that knowledge to your credentials.

The Query Design Environment

The query design environment, as seen in Figure 5-1, has two panes. The upper pane displays a graphical representation of the table or tables from which the query will retrieve data and, if multiple tables are included, it also shows the relationships between them. The lower pane contains the design grid. The fields included in the grid are displayed in the query's Datasheet view. You can also set criteria to select the records you want to view.

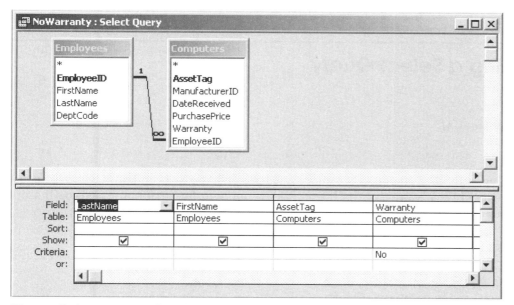

Figure 5-1: *An example of the query design environment.*

Examine a Select Query

Definition:

You use queries in Access to view, change, and analyze data in many different types of ways. A *select query* is the mostly commonly used type of query in Access.

A select query retrieves data from one or more tables and enables you to ask questions about your data. You select what fields you want to view and can use criteria to select records. You can also use a select query to group records and perform summary calculations.

Example:

If you had a database containing information on employees, you might use a select query to produce a list of employees who work less than 40 hours per week. Or you might want to list just the people who work in a certain department.

ACTIVITY 5-1

Examining a Select Query

Data Files:

- SelectQueries.mdb

Scenario:

You're working with your computer inventory database and you need to know which computers are not covered by a warranty. You'll use a select query to find that out. Then you'll see which ones are covered.

What You Do	How You Do It
1. From the My Documents folder, **open the SelectQueries database.** This is a copy of the database you designed and implemented to track computer inventory; some sample data has been provided. **Display the list of queries.**	a. **Click Open.** b. If necessary, in the Places bar, **select My Documents.** c. **Double-click on SelectQueries.** d. In the Database window, in the Objects bar, **select Queries.**
2. **Open the NoWarranty query and observe the datasheet.** This query displays a list of employees who are assigned computers that are not covered by a warranty. There are seven records displayed as indicated to the right of the Navigation bar. **Change to Design view.**	a. **Double-click on NoWarranty.** b. **Observe the datasheet.** c. **Click Design View.**
3. **Observe the design of the query.** The upper pane shows that it combines data from the Employees and Computers tables. The lower pane or design grid shows that it selects the LastName, FirstName, AssetTag, and Warranty fields. The criteria of No for the Warranty field selects only records where the value in that field is equal to No.	
4. **Change the criteria in the Warranty field to Yes and run the query again.**	a. In the design grid, in the Criteria row of the Warranty field, **select the value No.** b. **Type** *Yes.* c. **Click Datasheet View.**
5. **Observe the datasheet.** Now there are 19 records displayed and all have a value of Yes in the Warranty field.	

6. Close the datasheet window without saving changes to the design of the query.

    a. Click Close.

    b. Click No.

TOPIC B

Create a Query Using a Wizard

Now that you're familiar with how to run a query and what the design environment looks like, you'll create a new query by using a wizard.

Wizards in Access can be a fast way to get you all or part of the way to your desired outcome.

Create a Query Using a Wizard

Procedure Reference: Create a Query Using a Wizard

To create a query using a wizard:

1. In the Database window, in the Objects bar, select Queries.

2. Double-click on Create Query By Using Wizard.

3. Select the first table (or query) you wish to include in the query.

4. Add the Available Fields you wish to include to the Selected Fields list.

5. Repeat steps 3 and 4 if you want to include any additional tables (or queries).

6. Click Next.

7. If you've included a Numeric or Currency field in the query, you can select whether you want to view detail or summary information. If you select Summary, you can also set certain Summary Options.

   Click Next.

8. Enter a title for the query and select whether you want to open the query in Datasheet view or Design view.

9. Click Finish.

Data Sources for a Query

Queries can be based on one table, multiple tables as long as they have a relationship or can be related, or on another query.

ACTIVITY 5-2

Creating a Query Using a Wizard

Setup:

The SelectQueries database is open and Queries is selected in the Objects bar.

Scenario:

Imagine that you would like to see a list of your computers that includes the manufacturer, date received, and purchase price. You know you'll need to include fields from both the Computers and Manufacturers tables. Since you've used wizards to do a number of other things in Access, you decide to try one for the query you need to create to get this data.

What You Do	How You Do It
1. **Start the Simple Query Wizard.**	a. In the Database window, **double-click on Create Query By Using Wizard.**
2. **From the Computers table, add the AssetTag, DateReceived, and PurchasePrice fields.**	a. **Verify that Table: Computers is displayed in the Tables/Queries box.**
	b. If necessary, in the Available Fields list, **select AssetTag.**
	c. **Click on the rightward-pointing arrow** to add the field to the Selected Fields list.
	d. In the Available Fields list, **select DateReceived.**
	e. **Click on the rightward-pointing arrow.**
	f. In the Available Fields list, **select PurchasePrice.**
	g. **Click on the rightward-pointing arrow.**
3. **Now, from the Manufacturers table, add the Manufacturer field to the query and continue with the wizard.**	a. **Open the Tables/Queries drop-down list and select Table: Manufacturers.**
	b. In the Available Fields list, **select Manufacturer.**
	c. **Click on the rightward-pointing arrow.**
	d. **Click Next.**

4. Indicate that you want to see the detail records and continue with the wizard.	a. Verify that Detail is selected.
	b. Click Next.
5. Give your query a title of *MyBrands* and view the information.	a. In the title box, type *MyBrands*.
	b. Verify that Open The Query To View Information is selected.
	c. Click Finish.
6. **Observe the datasheet.** The fields you chose are displayed and the records appear to be sorted by Manufacturer names.	
7. Let's take a look at the design created by the wizard. **Change to Design view.**	a. Click Design View.
8. **Observe the query design.** The two tables are displayed and are joined on the ManufacturerID field. The fields you selected in the wizard are in the design grid.	
9. Close the query Design window.	a. Click Close.

Topic C

Work in Query Design View

The wizard was fast and easy, but did you notice that—in the wizard—you could select what fields you wanted to include but there was no opportunity to specify criteria to select only certain records? You also couldn't designate the order in which you wanted the records sorted. To get exactly the results you want, you need to work in Query Design view.

Select queries enable you to work with just the fields and records you want. To display just what you want the way you want it, you'll need to be able to create or modify queries in Design view.

Work in Query Design View

There are several techniques you can use to add fields to the design grid. You can:

- Double-click on a field in the graphic of the table in the upper pane.
- Click and drag a field to a column in the design grid.
- Select multiple fields in the graphic of the table by using the [Shift]-click or [Ctrl]-click techniques and drag them to the design grid.

- Add all the fields in a table to the design grid, by double-clicking on or dragging the asterisk (*) in the graphic of the table.

Join Tables

If tables do not have an established relationship and so are not automatically joined by Access when you include them in a query, you can join them temporarily by dragging the appropriate field from one table to the other. To join tables, the fields must be of the same or a compatible data type and must contain similar data.

Sort Records in a Query

The Sort row of the design grid enables you to sort the records in Ascending or Descending order. If you sort on more than one field, the sort will be performed on the fields in the order in which the fields are arranged from left to right in the design grid.

ACTIVITY 5-3

Working in Query Design View

Scenario:

You need to build some queries that you think you may want to run routinely, but you're not sure exactly what you need—so you're going to experiment a bit. The first thing you want is a list of employees.

What You Do	How You Do It
1. **Open the Design view for a new query and add the Employees table to the query.**	a. In the Database window, **double-click on Create Query In Design View.**
	b. On the Tables tab of the Show Table dialog box, **select Employees.**
	c. **Click Add.**
	d. **Click Close.**
2. **Using two different techniques, add the LastName and FirstName fields to the design grid, and then run the query.**	a. In the Employees table, **select the LastName field.**
	b. **Drag the field to the Field row in the first column in the design grid.**
	c. In the Employees table, **double-click on First Name.** The field is added to the next column.
	d. **Click Datasheet View.**

3. **Observe the datasheet.** It may appear that the records are in random order, but, actually, they're sorted by the primary key, EmployeeID.

4. You decide you want to sort the records by name. **Switch to Design view, sort the records by LastName and then by FirstName, and then run the query again.** When you get the correct results, **save the query as** *MyNameList*.

   a. **Click Design View.**

   b. In the LastName column, **click in the Sort row.**

   c. **Open the drop-down list and select Ascending.**

   d. In the FirstName column, **click in the Sort row.**

   e. **Open the drop-down list and select Ascending.**

   f. **Click Datasheet View.**

   g. **Click Save.**

   h. In the Query Name box, **type** *MyNameList*.

   i. **Click OK.**

5. Now you decide you'd like to add each person's department to the list before the name and have the first sort be on the department. **Switch to Design view and display the Show Table dialog box. Add the Departments table to the query.**

   Add the Department field as the first field in the design grid and choose an Ascending sort. Run the query to see if you get the results you want. If so, save the query as *MyDepartmentList*.

   ⚠ Remember that this query has been named and saved already so you'll have to choose File→Save As to give it a new name.

   a. **Click Design View.**

   b. **Click the Show Table** **button.**

   c. In the list of tables, **double-click on Departments.**

   d. **Click Close.**

   e. In the Departments table, **select the Department field.**

   f. **Drag the Department field on top of the LastName field in the design grid.** When you release the mouse button, the existing fields are moved to the right.

   g. **Click in the Sort row for the Department field.**

   h. **Open the Sort drop-down list and choose Ascending.**

   i. **Click Datasheet View.**

   j. **Choose File→Save As and name the query** *MyDepartmentList*.

   k. **Click OK.**

6. The two tables in the previous step were automatically joined in the query design because a relationship had been established between them. Now imagine that someone else in the company has an Access table containing office phone numbers and that person imported it to your database for you. You decide you'd like to add the phones to your list. **Add the Phones table to the design of the query.**

   a. **Click Design View.**

   b. **Click the Show Table button.**

   c. **Double-click on Phones.**

   d. **Click Close.**

7. **Observe the tables in the query design.** Because there was no relationship established between the Employees and Phones tables and because there is no common field with the same name, the tables are not automatically joined. So you'll have to do it manually.

8. **Try sizing the window and panes and arranging the tables in the diagram to make it easier to work with. Create a join between the Employees and Phones tables on the common field.**

   Add the OfficePhone field to the design grid and run the query, and then save the revised query as *MyPhoneList* and close the query window.

    You can size the columns in the design grid with the same techniques you use to size columns in a datasheet.

a. **Place the mouse pointer over the bottom edge of the query Design window until it becomes a vertical double-headed arrow.**

b. **Drag the bottom edge of the window down.**

c. **Place the mouse pointer over the divider between the upper and lower panes until it becomes a horizontal line with a vertical double-headed arrow.**

d. **Drag the divider down.**

e. **Move the Phone table in the diagram by dragging it by its title bar. Place it below the Departments table.**

f. **To create a join between the Employees and Phones tables, drag the EmployeeID field to the EmpID field in the diagram.**

g. **In the Phones table, double-click on OfficePhone.**

h. **Click Datasheet View.**

i. **Choose File→Save As and name the query *MyPhoneList*.**

j. **Click OK.**

k. **Click Close.**

TOPIC D

Select Records

Now you know how to add fields and tables in the design of a query, and the results you saw included all of the records from the underlying tables. Many times, however, you will want to work with only a portion of your records. For example, you might want to view the records for an employee who works in a particular department, orders that were placed in a certain time frame, or records that have no value in a field so you can update them. That's what this topic is all about.

Using criteria to select just the records you want is a technique you will use to answer many business questions. How many computers did you buy in 2000? How many cost more than $1,500? These are just a couple of examples of the questions you'll need to answer every day by querying your data.

Operators

The following comparison operators can be used in setting criteria in a query: If you don't enter an operator, Access assumes = (equal).

Operator	Meaning
>	greater than
<	less than
>=	greater than or equal to
<=	less than or equal to
< >	not equal to

The Between Operator

The Between operator can be used to set criteria for a field of a Date/Time data type. For example, entering the criteria Between 2/1/01 And 2/15/01 will retrieve records with values of 2/1/01 through 2/15/01.

The Null Operator

The Null operator can be used to select records that do not contain a value in a field. Enter *Is Null* as the criteria to select records with no value and enter *Is Not Null* to select only records that do contain a value.

AND and OR conditions

To retrieve just the records you want to view, you can enter more than one criteria on the same or different fields. If, for example, you are using two criteria on different fields and enter them on the same Criteria row of the design grid, they constitute an AND condition. This means that **both** criteria must be met by each record in order for the record to be returned by the query. An AND condition is created on one field by including the word "AND" in the criteria as in ">2000 and <4000".

An OR condition means that **either** of the criteria you set must be met. You create an OR condition on one field by including the word "OR." To create an OR condition on different fields, enter one criteria on the Criteria row of the design grid and the second criteria on the Or row.

An AND condition is more restrictive than an OR condition, because all criteria must be met so an AND condition will return fewer records.

 Criteria entered on the same Criteria or Or row of the design grid automatically form an AND condition.

Select Records

Procedure Reference: Select Specific Records in a Query

To select specific records in a query:

1. In the design grid, include the field or fields for which you want to set criteria.

2. Enter the first criteria in the Criteria row for the field.

   If you want to create an AND or OR condition on a single field, include the appropriate word in the criteria.

3. To create an AND condition on more than one field, enter the other criteria on the same Criteria row.

4. To create an OR condition on more than one field, enter the other criteria on the Or row.

The Show Box

In the design grid, there is a Show row with a checkbox for each field in the query. By default, the Show box is checked and the field is displayed in Datasheet view of the query. You may want to include a field in the design grid in order to set criteria on the field but you may not want that field displayed in the datasheet. In that event, uncheck the Show box.

ACTIVITY 5-4

Selecting Records

Scenario:

The company President has asked you to demonstrate the ways you can extract data from your new database. She's interested in understanding what types of analyses can be done and what business information is available that the company never had easy access to before.

What You Do	How You Do It
1. Open the Inventory query and observe the data and note the number of records.	a. In the Database window, **double-click on Inventory.**
	b. Observe the data and note that there are 23 records.
2. If you wanted to know which computers cost more than $2,000, you can answer that question with a comparison operator. Switch to **Design** view and enter the appropriate criteria. Run the query and see how many records satisfy that condition.	a. Click Design View.
	b. Scroll to view the PurchasePrice field in the design grid.
	c. Click in the Criteria row for the PurchasePrice field.
	d. Type *>2000*.
	e. Click Datasheet View.
	f. Note that six records satisfy the condition.

3. Say that you wanted to know how many computers are assigned to the Technical Services department. Since both the DeptCode and Department fields are included in the query, you can use either to set the criteria.

In Design view, **remove the PurchasePrice criteria and set a condition that the DeptCode be equal to 500. Choose to not display the DeptCode field in the query datasheet, and then run the query.**

📌 You do not have to enter the equal sign (=) in the criteria (it's assumed), and you do not have to display the field you use to set a condition.

a. **Switch to Design view.**

b. In the PurchasePrice field, **select and delete the >2000 criteria.**

c. **Click in the Criteria row for the DeptCode field.**

d. **Type** *500*.

e. **In the Show row, uncheck the box for the DeptCode field.**

f. **Click Datasheet View and observe the data.**

---

4. You can use multiple criteria to select records. **Enter the appropriate criteria to find out how many Atlas computers are assigned to Technical Services.**

a. **Switch to Design view.**

b. **Click in the Criteria row for the Manufacturer field.**

c. **Type** *Atlas*.

d. **Click Datasheet View.**

---

5. **Observe the data.** Only two records satisfy this condition. By entering two conditions on the same Criteria row in the design grid, you create an AND condition and records must satisfy both conditions to be displayed in the query datasheet.

---

6. The next question you want to answer was how many computers are assigned to the Technical Services department or are made by Cyber (and assigned to any department). **Enter the appropriate criteria, run the query, and see how many records are displayed.**

📌 Remember that you can create AND and OR conditions for the same field by including those operators in the criteria. For example, if you wanted to know how many Atlas and Cyber computers you have, you can enter the criteria "Atlas and Cyber."

a. **Switch to Design view.**

b. **Delete the condition on the Criteria row of the Manufacturer field.**

c. **Click in the Or row of the Manufacturer field.**

d. **Type** *Cyber*.

e. **Run the query.**

---

7. **Observe the 10 records that are displayed.** All computers assigned to the Technical Services department are included, as well as records for Cyber computers assigned to any department.

---

8. Now the President asks you how many computers were acquired during the first quarter of 2001. **Use the Between operator to create that criteria and run the query.** Six records should be displayed.

📌 Access automatically enters numbers signs (#) around date values.

    a. **Switch to Design view.**

    b. **Delete the Cyber and 500 criteria.**

    c. **Click in the Criteria row for the DateReceived field.**

    d. **Type *Between 1/1/2001 And 3/31/2001*.**

    e. **Run the query and verify that six records are displayed.**

9. You know that occasionally the person doing data entry doesn't know the manufacturer of the computer when the record is first entered. You want to see if there are any missing values so you can follow-up and get that information. You only need the employee and computer information so **delete the Departments and Manufacturers tables from the query. Use the Null operator to create a criteria in the ManufacturerID field of the Computers table** to locate records with a blank value.

When you get the correct results (three records), **save the query with the new name *MyMissingValues* and close the query window.**

    a. **Switch to Design view.**

    b. **In the upper pane, right-click on the Departments table.**

    c. **Choose Remove Table.**

    d. **Remove the Manufacturers table from the query.**

    e. **Delete the criteria in the DateReceived field.**

    f. **In the Criteria row for the ManufacturerID field, type *Is Null*.**

    g. **Run the query.**

    h. **Choose File→Save As, type *MyMissingValues*, and click OK.**

    i. **Close the query window.**

TOPIC E

Edit Values in a Query Datasheet

Queries are not just for selecting and viewing data. You can also use the query datasheet to enter and edit values, so that's what you'll do next.

Since many databases have hundreds or thousands of records, it can be time-consuming to search through those records when you need to enter or edit information. One efficient technique is to use a query to display the records you need to change.

Edit Values in a Query Datasheet

Procedure Reference: Edit Values Using a Select Query

To use a select query to edit values:

1. Create a select query that includes the table or tables with values you wish to edit.

2. Include the necessary field(s) in the design grid.

3. Enter criteria to select the record or records whose values you wish to edit.

4. Edit the values.

Updateable Data

Not all data displayed in a query Datasheet view can always be updated. All fields in a query based on one table can be updated, as can fields in a query based on tables with a one-to-one relationship; however, in a query based on tables with a one-to-many relationship, certain fields are not updateable. See the Access Help topic "When Can I Update Data From A Query?" for additional information.

ACTIVITY 5-5

Editing Values in a Query Datasheet

Scenario:

Data in a database only has value as information if it's accurate, so data maintenance is an important task. You want to make sure that the data in your computer inventory database is as up to date and accurate as possible. One of your regular tasks is to check for missing information and complete those records.

What You Do	How You Do It
1. **Open the Updates query.** This is like the query you created earlier to locate computer records that don't have a ManufacturerID. **Enter the following ManufacturerID values and be sure that each record is saved.**	a. In the Database window, **double-click on the Updates query.**
	b. **Move the insertion point to the ManufacturerID field for the first record.**
	c. Using the ManufacturerID values shown on the left, **enter a value.**
	d. **Press the down arrow.** Using the down arrow key keeps the insertion point in the same column.
	e. **Enter a value for this and the next record.**
	f. **Move off the last record to save the change.**
2. As you're looking at the data, you notice that Lynne McMillan's first name is misspelled. **Edit her record to the correct spelling, save the record, and then close the query datasheet.**	a. **Place the insertion point at the end of the value Lyn.**
	b. **Type** *ne*.
	c. **Move off the record to save the change.**
	d. **Close the query datasheet.**

LastName	FirstName	AssetTag	ManufacturerID
Coleman	William	1215	3
Haygood	Eric	1044	1
McMillan	Lyn	1075	4

3. Let's prove to ourselves that the changes we made to the data were indeed saved in the underlying tables. **Open the Employees table, find the McMillan record, and verify that the corrected first name is displayed. Close the table when done.**

   a. In the Database window, **display the list of tables.**

   b. **Open the Employees table.**

   c. **Find the record with a last name of McMillan.**

   d. **Verify the corrected first name.**

   e. **Close the Employees table.**

4. Now check the records about the computers. **Open the Computers table and, using the information in the graphic that follows, locate the records and verify that the values you entered are displayed in the ManufacturerID field. Close the table when done.**

   a. **Open the Computers table.**

   b. **Find the record for the computer with AssetTag 1215.**

   c. **Verify that the value you entered is displayed in the ManufacturerID field.**

   d. **Refer to the graphic, locate the other records you updated, and verify that the values are displayed.**

   e. **Close the Computers table.**

LastName	FirstName	AssetTag	ManufacturerID
Coleman	William	1215	3
Haygood	Eric	1044	1
McMillan	Lyn	1075	4

TOPIC F
Add a Calculated Field to a Query

When you planned your database, you intentionally did not include any fields to store data that could be calculated from other fields. Often, you'll do those calculations in a query, so that's what you'll work on in this topic.

Queries are very powerful in Access and can save you time and work by enabling you to quickly do calculations on all the records in your database. You might want to total or average certain data or be able to do projections.

Creating Expressions

An expression is a formula for a calculation. When you need to enter an expression, you can type it in directly if you know the exact field names and syntax. Or you can use the Expression Builder, seen in Figure 5-2, to help you.

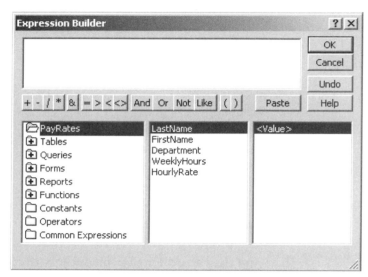

Figure 5-2: *The Expression Builder.*

The common arithmetic operators shown in Table 5-1 are used in creating calculated expressions in Access.

Table 5-1: *Arithmetic Operators*

Operator	Meaning
+	add
-	subtract
/	divide
*	multiply

Add a Calculated Field to a Query

Procedure Reference: Create a Calculated Field Using the Expression Builder

To create a calculated field using the Expression Builder:

1. In the query design grid, right-click in the first available blank column.

2. Choose Build.

3. Using the operator bar and the lists of fields and functions, select and paste each component of the expression.

4. Click OK to enter the expression in the design grid.

Name a Calculated Field

When you create a calculated field in the design grid, Access automatically assigns it a name such as "Expr1." You can enter your own name for the calculated field before you create the expression, or you can change the name assigned by Access to something more meaningful. In the design grid, the calculated field name must be followed by a colon (:).

Opening the Zoom Box

When working in the design grid, you may not be able to view all the contents of a column, such as the expression for a calculated field. You can widen the column or you can open the Zoom box to see the entire contents. To open the Zoom box, right-click on the field and choose Zoom.

Field Properties

Each field in a query has properties associated with it; the properties available depend on the data type of the field. For example, for a numeric field, commonly used properties are Format and Decimal Places. To view and set the properties for a field, right-click on the field and choose Properties.

ACTIVITY 5-6

Adding a Calculated Field to a Query

Scenario:

Imagine that your database contains a lot of numeric data and you often need to do various analyses of that data. You have a table in your database that includes data on employees' weekly work hours and hourly pay rates. The types of calculations you need to do involve existing fields to arrive at new data and what-if calculations. So you will calculate the weekly gross pay for all employees, enter a name for the calculated field, and use the Format property to change the display format of the results.

What You Do	How You Do It
1. **Open the PayRates query in Design view and observe the design. Run the query.**	a. In the Database window, **display the list of queries.**
	b. **Right-click on the PayRates query.**
	c. **Choose Design View.**
	d. **Observe the design.** It includes an HoursAndRates table and will display a list of employees and their hours and rates.
	e. **Click Datasheet View** to run the query.

2. You've been asked to calculate the weekly gross pay for all employees. **Switch to Design view. Right-click in the next blank column in the design grid. Use the Expression Builder to create the correct arithmetic expression. Run the query and check the calculation.**

   a. **Switch to Design view.**

   b. In the design grid, **right-click in the next blank column and choose Build.**

   c. In the Expression Builder Operator bar, **click the equal sign (=).**

   d. In the field list (the middle column), **double-click on WeeklyHours.** Notice that the field name is added to the expression and is enclosed in brackets.

   e. In the Operator bar, **click the multiplication sign (*).**

   f. In the field list, **double-click on HourlyRate.**

   g. **Click OK.**

   h. **Run the query.**

3. **Observe the results.** Did you get a value of 760 for Rob Abbott? Notice that the calculated field has a column heading of Expr1 and the values have a general number format.

4. **Switch to Design view and observe the column for the calculated field.** It was automatically named "Expr1."

5. **Open the Zoom dialog box and change the name of the calculated field to *WeeklyGross*. Run the query to verify that the name is displayed as the column heading.**

   a. **Right-click on the calculated field and choose Zoom.**

   b. **Select Expr1 and type *WeeklyGross*.**

    Make sure you have a colon (:) after WeeklyGross.

   c. **Click OK.**

   d. **Run the query.**

   e. **Verify that WeeklyGross is displayed as the column heading.**

6. Switch to Design view. Open the Field Properties dialog box for the WeeklyGross field and set the Format property to Currency. Run the query and observe the new format.	a. Switch to Design view.
	b. Right-click on the WeeklyGross field and choose Properties.
	c. Click in the Format property box.
	d. Open the drop-down list and select Currency.
	e. Close the Field Properties dialog box.
	f. Run the query.
	g. Observe that the calculated values are displayed in currency format.
7. Save the revised query as *MyWeeklyGross*.	a. Choose File→Save As.
	b. Type *MyWeeklyGross*.
	c. Click OK.

OPTIONAL PRACTICE ACTIVITY 5-7

Using Calculations for Projections

Scenario:

You've been asked to calculate what each employee's hourly rate would be if everyone was given a 3 percent increase.

1. If necessary, **open the MyWeeklyGross query in Design view.**

2. **Create a calculated field named *NewRate* with the appropriate arithmetic expression.**

3. **Format the calculated field as Currency.**

4. Run the query and check your results against the following graphic.

	LastName	FirstName	Department	WeeklyHours	HourlyRate	WeeklyGross	NewRate
▶	Abbott	Rob	Technical Services	40.0	$19.00	$760.00	$19.57
	Aktasi	Goodwin	Fulfillment	40.0	$15.00	$600.00	$15.45
	Andres	Leon	Finance	32.5	$12.50	$406.25	$12.88
	Atkinson	Angela	Sales	35.0	$17.25	$603.75	$17.77
	Ballantyne	Carl	Administration	40.0	$13.95	$558.00	$14.37
	Barefoot	Karen	Sales	40.0	$22.00	$880.00	$22.66
	Barnett	Amy	Administration	40.0	$14.50	$580.00	$14.94
	Barrows	Helene	Technical Services	40.0	$10.00	$400.00	$10.30
	Bernstein	Edward	Sales	40.0	$12.00	$480.00	$12.36
	Bonafede	Mike	Sales	40.0	$15.00	$600.00	$15.45
	Brown	Andrea	Finance	37.5	$18.50	$693.75	$19.06
	Byam	Vishna	Sales	40.0	$23.20	$928.00	$23.90
	Caldwell	Josh	Fulfillment	37.5	$18.00	$675.00	$18.54

MyWeeklyGross : Select Query

5. Save the query as *MyNewRates* and close the query datasheet.

TOPIC G

Perform a Calculation for a Group of Records

The calculations you've done so far resulted in a new column holding a new value for every record in the datasheet. You might think of it as a horizontal calculation. Another type of calculation is one that works in a vertical direction—some kind of summary calculation for all records or groups of records. That's what this topic is about.

With all the data in a database, it's easy to get lost in the details. Summary calculations enable you to give a big picture view of large amounts of data.

Perform a Calculation for a Group of Records

Procedure Reference: Perform a Summary Calculation for a Group of Records

To perform a summary calculation for a group of records:

1. To the design grid, add the field(s) on which you want to group records and the field(s) you wish to summarize.

2. Click the Totals button to display the Total row.

3. Enter any criteria necessary to select the records you wish to view.

   If you need to enter criteria for a field on which you are not grouping records, include that field in the design grid and select Where from the Total drop-down list.

4. For each field, open the Total drop-down list and choose Group By or the summary function.

5. Run the query.

The Total Row

When you display the Total row in the design grid by clicking the Totals button, each field included in the grid must have an entry in that row. Normally, you should include just the fields on which you want to group the records and the fields on which you want to perform the summary calculation. The Totals button is a toggle that turns the display of the Total row on and off.

Summary Functions

The following are the summary functions available when using the Total row:

- SUM: totals the values
- AVG: averages all values (excludes null values from calculation)
- MIN: returns the smallest value
- MAX: returns the largest value
- COUNT: counts the number of values
- STDEV: calculates the standard deviation
- VAR: calculates the variance
- FIRST: returns the first record entered according to chronological order
- LAST: returns the last record entered

ACTIVITY 5-8

Performing a Calculation for a Group of Records

Scenario:

Now you've been asked to provide the average weekly hours for employees in each department and the total weekly gross payroll for each department. And the information is needed now!

What You Do	How You Do It
1. If necessary, **close any open datasheet windows. Open the WeeklyInfo query and observe the data.**	a. If necessary, **close any open datasheet windows.**
	b. **Double-click on WeeklyInfo.**
	c. **Observe the data.**
2. **Switch to Design view and add the Total row to the design grid.**	a. **Switch to Design view.**
	b. **Click the Totals button** $\boxed{\Sigma}$ **.**

3. **Observe the design grid.** The Total row is displayed and Group By is entered for each field.

4. Since you want to group the data on departments, not individuals, **remove the LastName and FirstName fields from the design grid.**

   a. In the design grid, **place the mouse pointer over the selector for the LastName field until it becomes a downward-pointing arrow.**

   b. **Click to select the field.**

   c. **Press [Delete].**

   d. **Select and delete the FirstName field.**

5. In the Total row for the WeeklyHours field, **enter the appropriate summary function to calculate the average weekly hours for each department.**

   a. **Click in the Total row for the WeeklyHours field.**

   b. **Open the drop-down list and select Avg.**

6. In the Total row for the WeeklyGross field, **enter the appropriate summary function to calculate the total weekly payroll for each department.**

   Run the query.

   a. **Click in the Total row for the WeeklyGross field.**

   b. **Open the drop-down list and select Sum.**

   c. **Run the query.**

7. **Compare your results to the following graphic.**

WeeklyInfo : Select Query		
Department	AvgOfWeeklyHours	WeeklyGross
Administration	39.1666666666667	$4,066.00
Finance	36.6666666666667	$1,820.00
Fulfillment	38.7941176470588	$12,070.55
Sales	38.3846153846154	$9,126.95
Technical Services	39.1111111111111	$6,606.00

8. If necessary, **size the columns so you can see the full column headings.**

    Switch to Design view and format the WeeklyHours field so the average will be displayed with one decimal place.

    a. **Double-click on the right edge of any column heading you cannot view fully.**

    b. **Switch to Design view.**

    c. **Right-click on the WeeklyHours field and choose Properties.**

    d. **Click in the Format property box.**

    e. **Open the drop-down list and select Fixed.**

    f. **For the Decimal Places property, open the drop-down list and select 1.**

    g. **Close the Field Properties dialog box.**

9. **Run the query to check your results. Save the query as *MyTotals* and close the datasheet window.**

    a. **Run the query.**

    b. **Choose File→Save As.**

    c. **Type *MyTotals*.**

    d. **Click OK.**

    e. **Close the datasheet window.**

Lesson 5 Follow-up

Your data holds the answers to many questions. In order to find an answer, you have to ask a question, and building a query does just that. You can use the Query Wizard to create a query on the fly, or you can build a custom query in Design view. Adding operators and conditions allows you to sort your records to get at specified information, and adding calculated fields enables you to use existing data to make projections. As you have seen, queries give you the ability to discover the answers your data holds.

1. **What are some ways you might use queries in your databases?**

2. **Which query options do you think will be most useful in your work?**

NOTES

LESSON 6

Creating and Using Forms

Lesson Time
60 minutes

Lesson Objectives:

In this lesson, you will create and modify forms to work with your data.

You will:

- Create forms to display data by using the AutoForm feature.
- Create a new form using a wizard.
- Modify the design of a form to improve the display of data.
- Use forms to edit data.

Introduction

You will most often work with your data by viewing it in a form. There are several different ways you can create forms and this lesson will introduce you to the most commonly used techniques. You'll also have an opportunity to familiarize yourself with Form Design view and modify the design of a form by working with objects, properties, and commands. You'll then use forms to work with data.

You'll use both AutoForm and the Form Wizard to create forms quickly. Then you'll also see how to modify the design of forms to customize them to your needs and preferences. You'll then use forms to work with data.

TOPIC A

Create AutoForms

You've used wizards in Access to create tables and queries, but there's an even faster way to produce a form and that's by using the AutoForm feature. You'll use it to create two forms that illustrate how AutoForm works with different kinds of data.

By understanding your options for creating forms, you'll be able to choose the one that best meets your needs. AutoForm is the fastest means for creating a form.

Create AutoForms

Procedure Reference: Create an AutoForm

An AutoForm displays the fields from one record at a time with the field names and fields arranged in columns.

If you create an AutoForm for a table that is not related to any other tables in the database, only the records from that table are displayed in the form. If you create an AutoForm for a table that has an established relationship with one or more other tables, related records from those tables are displayed in subdatasheets.

To create an AutoForm:

1. In the Database window, in the Objects bar, select Tables.

2. Select the table for which you want to create an AutoForm.

3. Click the NewObject: AutoForm button.

ACTIVITY 6-1

Creating Forms with AutoForm

Data Files:

- UseForms.mdb

Scenario:

Imagine that you've never created forms for your database before, but you're leaving on vacation and want to provide some forms for the person who will doing data maintenance while you're gone. You decide to use the AutoForm feature.

What You Do	How You Do It
1. From the My Documents folder, **open the UseForms database and select the Customers table.** This table is not related to any other data in the database.	a. **Click Open.**
	b. **Double-click on UseForms.**
	c. In the list of tables, **select Customers.**

📌 When using AutoForm to create a form to display data in a table with no related data, first select the table in the Database window.

2. **Create an AutoForm based on the Customers table.**	a. **Click the NewObject: AutoForm button** 🗃 .

3. **Observe the new form.** All the fields in the table are arranged in the form in a columnar layout. The name of the table is displayed in the title bar.

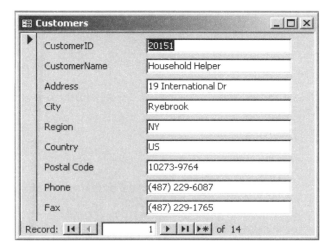

4. **Close and save the form with the name *MyCustomers*.**

    a. **Click Close.**

    b. **Click Yes.**

    c. Type *MyCustomers*.

    d. **Click OK.**

5. Now you'll create an AutoForm for a table that is related to another table in the database. **Create an AutoForm based on the Employees table.**

    a. In the list of tables, **select Employees.**

    b. **Click the New Object: AutoForm button.**

6. **Observe the new form.** The fields in the table you selected are arranged in the form in a columnar layout and the name of that table is displayed in the title bar. Data from the related table is displayed as a datasheet with the expand indicator (+) for a subdatasheet.

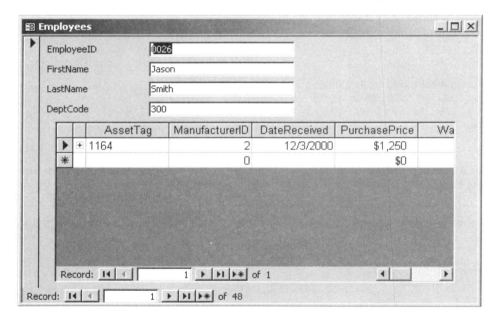

There are navigation bars for both the form and the datasheet. Also, note that the form is not quite wide enough to display all the fields.

7. **Expand and observe the subdatasheet.** Related data from a third table is displayed. **Close the subdatasheet.**

    a. **Click the expand indicator (+).**

    b. **Notice that related data from a third table is displayed.**

    c. **Click the collapse indicator (-).**

8. **Widen the form window and attempt to widen the datasheet.** You can make the form window wider but not the datasheet—that has to be adjusted in Form Design view.

   a. **Place the mouse pointer over the right side of the form window until it becomes a horizontal double-headed arrow.**

   b. **Click and drag the right edge of the form window to the right.**

   c. **Place the mouse pointer over the right edge of the datasheet.** The horizontal sizing pointer is not displayed; the size of the datasheet must be adjusted in Form Design view.

9. **Save the form as *MyEmployees* and close the form.**

   a. **Click Save.**

   b. **Type *MyEmployees*.**

   c. **Click OK.**

   d. **Click Close.**

Topic B

Create a Form Using a Wizard

Now that you've seen what AutoForm can do for you, you'll use the same data example and use a wizard to create a form. This will give you an opportunity to compare how these two features work so you can decide which to use when.

Whenever you need to create a form, using a wizard to get started is almost always a time-saver. Then, if necessary, you can go on to customize the form.

Create a Form Using a Wizard

Procedure Reference: Create a Form Using a Wizard

To create a form using a wizard:

1. In the Database window, in the Objects bar, select Forms.

2. Double-click on Create Form By Using Wizard.

3. Use the Tables/Queries drop-down list to select the first data source for the form.

4. Add the fields you want in the form to the Selected Fields list.

5. Repeat steps 3 and 4 for any additional data sources and fields. Click Next.

6. If you have fields from more than one table, decide how you want the wizard to organize it. Then decide whether you want subforms or linked forms for the related data. Click Next.

7. Choose the form layout and click Next.

8. Choose the form style and click Next.

9. Enter a title for the form and, if necessary, the subform. Select the view in which you want to open the form. Click Finish.

Subforms and Linked Forms

A subform displays related data within the main form. A linked form requires that you click a command button to open another form to display the related data.

Form Layouts

In the wizard, the available layouts for a form are: Columnar, Tabular, Datasheet, Justi-fied, PivotTable, and PivotChart. The preview provides an idea of what each looks like. If you're not sure which best suits your data, make your best guess; if the results are not what you want, you can always delete the form in the Database window and try again.

Form Styles

The form styles determine the overall look of a form, including the background and the color and font of labels and the data. It is suggested that you use the same style for all the forms in a database.

Form Title

In the wizard, you assign a title for the form and any related subforms. By default, the name you enter is used as the object name in the Database window, and it is displayed in the title bar for the form.

ACTIVITY 6-2

Creating a Form Using a Wizard

Scenario:

You would like a form that has a different look and is a bit more customized to how you want to view the data. You decide to try out the Form Wizard.

What You Do	How You Do It
1. **Display form objects and start the Form Wizard.**	a. In the Objects bar, **select Forms.**
	b. **Double-click on Create Form By Using Wizard.**
2. From the Employees table, **add all the fields to the Selected Fields list for the form.** From the Computers table, **add the AssetTag, DateReceived, PurchasePrice, and Warranty fields to the Selected Fields list. Continue with the wizard.**	a. In the Tables/Queries drop-down list, **select Table: Employees.**
	b. **Click on the rightward-pointing double arrows** `>>` . This adds all the fields in the table to the Selected Fields list.
	c. In the Tables/Queries drop-down list, **select Table: Computers.**
	d. In the Available Fields list, **verify that AssetTag is selected.**
	e. **Click on the rightward-pointing arrow.**
	f. In the Available Fields list, **select DateReceived.**
	g. **Click the rightward-pointing arrow.**
	h. **Add the PurchasePrice and Warranty fields to the Selected Fields list.**
	i. **Click Next.**

3. The wizard recognizes that this is related data. First, you have to decide whether you want it organized by employees or by computers. Try the two choices and observe the preview of the form. Then select By Employees.

   The second decision is whether you want a form with subforms or linked forms. Try the two options and observe the preview of the form. Select the option that will enable you to open only one form, and then continue with the wizard.

   a. Observe the preview of the form when organized By Employees.

   b. Select By Computers and observe the preview.

   c. Select By Employees.

   d. Verify that Form With Subform(s) is selected and observe the preview.

   e. Select Linked Forms and observe the preview.

   f. Select Form With Subform(s).

   g. Click Next.

4. Now you can choose the layout. Observe the preview for the Datasheet layout. Select Tabular, observe the preview, and then continue with the wizard.

   a. Observe the preview for the Datasheet layout.

   b. Select Tabular.

   c. Observe the preview.

   d. Click Next.

5. Observe the preview of the various styles available. Select the style you prefer and continue with the wizard.

   a. In the list of styles, select each style and observe the preview.

   b. Select the style you prefer.

   c. Click Next.

6. Give the form a title of *MyEmployees2* and the subform *MyComputers Subform*. Open the form.

   a. In the Form text box, type *MyEmployees2*.

   b. In the Subform text box, type *MyComputers Subform*.

   c. Verify that Open The Form To View Or Enter Information is selected.

   d. Click Finish.

7. **Observe the form.** The example that follows is in the Standard style. Because you chose the Tabular layout, the related records have the look of a form rather than a datasheet.

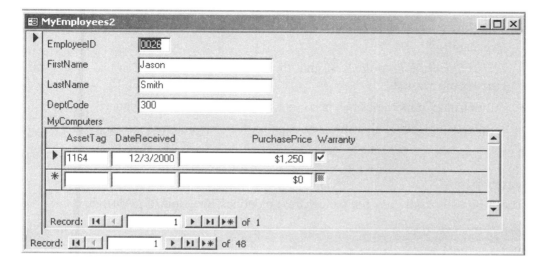

8. **Close the form.**   a. **Click Close.**

TOPIC C

Modify the Design of the Form

You've seen the results you can get with AutoForms and a sample of what the wizard can do. Now you'll have a chance to work in Form Design view and start changing the design of the form.

There are many changes you can make to a form in Form Design view and it's the only way to get a truly customized form that meets the needs and preferences of the user.

Form Design Principles

When designing a form, there are several things to consider. You must design with an eye toward practical matters such as the order of information, design elements such as use of space and size, and you should keep in mind basic composition and layout principles. With a little attention to these considerations, you can create a readable and usable form.

Good form design considers order of information, design elements, and composition and layout principles.

Guidelines

When designing a form, keep in mind the following guidelines.

- Information should be presented in an order that causes the eye to move naturally from the top of the form to the first item, to the second, then the third, and so on, all the way to the bottom of the form.
- Objects should be in balance with the space between them to maximize the form's readability.
- Size objects appropriately so that their contents can be read and so that space is not being wasted.
- Emphasize important objects so that they stand out at first glance.
- Balance objects so that they are equally distributed across the page.
- Group objects together in such a way that they look like they belong together.

Non-Example:

The following form does not follow the guidelines for good form design.

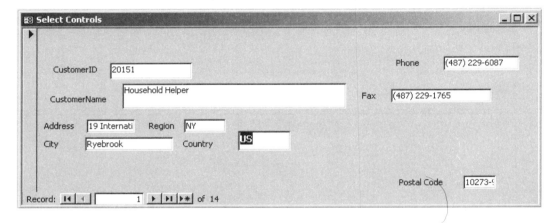

Example:

Here is a new version of the poorly designed form. As you can see, this form follows the guidelines for good form design.

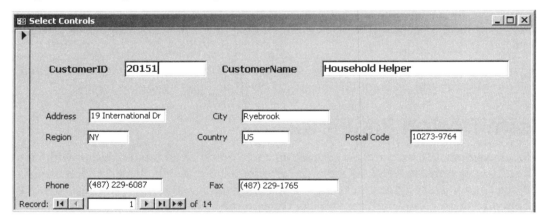

Tab Order of Controls

When you create a form, the order in which values are selected when you press [Tab] is determined by the initial placement of the controls on the form. This is referred to as the *tab order*. To change the tab order, choose View→Tab Order and follow the instructions in the dialog box. The Auto Order option will set the tab order of controls from left to right and top to bottom.

Select Controls

A control is any object on a form. Among others, you will find controls holding labels (often a field name) and text boxes that are commonly used to display the data from the table or query on which the form is based.

To make any changes to a control, you must first select it. It's just like formatting text in a word-processing application; you must select an item to affect it.

There are a number of techniques you can use to select one or more controls. You know a control is selected when the move handle is displayed in the upper-left corner and sizing handles are displayed as shown in the following graphic.

Depending on the situation, you can use the following methods to select the appropriate controls.

- To select a single control, click on the control.
- To select contiguous controls, click above and to the left of the controls and drag to enclose them in the rectangle. This is known as the lasso technique.
- To select all the controls in a horizontal or vertical line, click in the appropriate ruler.
- To select non-contiguous controls, click to select one control, press and hold down the [Shift] key, and click the other controls.

ACTIVITY 6-3

Selecting Controls

Activity Time:

5 minutes

Scenario:

You've decided you want to try customize a form but know that first you need to learn how to work in the form design environment. When you open a form in Design view, you realize that you need some practice in selecting the various controls that are on the form.

Lesson 6

What You Do	How You Do It
1. **Open the form SelectControls in Design view. Select the text box control holding the CustomerName field, and then select the label control for the field.** As you select each, notice the change in the selection handles.	a. In the Database window, **right-click on SelectControls and choose Design View.** b. **Click on the text box containing the CustomerName field.** Note that the control has selection handles on all sides. The accompanying label control has only a move handle in the upper-left corner. c. **Click on the label control for the CustomerName field.** Now, the label control has selection handles and the text box has only a move handle.
2. Using the lasso technique, in the top portion of the form, **select the customer ID, name, phone, and fax controls** and observe the selection handles.  **Deselect the controls.**	a. **Position the mouse pointer above and to the left of the CustomerID label.** b. **Click and drag to draw a rectangle that touches the CustomerID label in the upper left and the Fax text box in the lower right.** c. **Note that all the controls have selection handles.** d. **Click on a gray portion of the form** to deselect the controls.
3. Using the click-in-ruler technique, **select the labels and text boxes for the city, region, country, and postal code information. Observe the selection handles, and then deselect the controls.**	a. **Click in the vertical ruler at the 1.75-inch mark.** b. **Observe the selection handles.** c. **Click on a gray portion of the form** to deselect the controls.
4. Also, using the ruler, **select the labels and text boxes containing the customerID, phone, address, and city information. Observe the selection handles, and then deselect the controls.**	a. **Click at the 0.5-inch mark on the horizontal ruler.** b. **Click and drag to about the 1.5-inch mark.** c. **Observe the selection handles.** d. **Deselect the controls.**

5. Using the [Shift]-click technique, select the CustomerID, Fax, and PostalCode text box controls. Observe the selection handles, and then deselect the controls.

    a. Click on the CustomerID text box.

    b. Press and hold down the [Shift] key.

    c. Click on the Fax text box.

    d. Click on the PostalCode text box.

    e. Release the [Shift] key.

    f. Deselect the controls.

Size Controls

There are a number of techniques you can use to adjust the size of controls to better display their controls. After selecting a control, you can:

*   Drag a sizing handle to increase or decrease the size.

*   Choose Format→Size→To Fit.

*   Select multiple controls and choose Format→Size→To Tallest, To Shortest, To Widest, or To Narrowest. The same options available from the Format menu are available by right-clicking on a selected control and choosing Size from the shortcut menu.

ACTIVITY 6-4

Sizing Controls

Activity Time:

5 minutes

Setup:

The SelectControls form is open in Design view.

Scenario:

You've found that when you create an AutoForm or one with the wizard, the controls are not always the right size. Sometimes they're bigger than you need to display the data and occupy extra space on the form. Other times, they're not big enough and you can't view all of the data from a field. So you want to know how to make them the correct size.

What You Do	How You Do It
1. Switch to Form view and view the data in several records.	a. Click Form View.
	b. On the navigation bar, **click the Next button several times.**
2. **Observe the controls on the form.** Some controls, like the text boxes holding CustomerID and Fax data, are larger than they need to be to display the data. Others like the Address text box and the PostalCode label are too small and truncate the contents.	
3. **Switch to Design view and make the CustomerID text box approximately 0.5 inches wide and the Address text box 2 inches wide.**	a. Click on the CustomerID text box.
	b. Place the mouse pointer over the sizing handle in the middle of the right side of the text box until it becomes a horizontal double-headed arrow.
	c. Click and drag the sizing handle to the left until the text box is 0.5 inches wide (watch the horizontal ruler to judge the width).
	d. Click on the Address text box.
	e. Using the sizing handle on the right size, **click and drag to make the text box about 2 inches wide.**
4. **Size the PostalCode label to fit its contents.**	a. Click on the PostalCode label.
	b. Choose Format→Size→To Fit.
5. Using the menu bar, **make the CustomerID text box the height of the CustomerName text box.** Imagine you are unhappy with the new size and undo the sizing.	a. Click on the CustomerID text box.
	b. Press and hold down the [Shift] key and click on the Customer Name text box.
	c. Choose Format→Size→To Tallest.
	d. Click the Undo button ⟲ .
6. Using the shortcut menu, **make the Fax text box the same size as the Phone text box.**	a. Select the Fax and Phone text boxes.
	b. Right-click on one of the selected text boxes.
	c. Choose Size→To Narrowest.

| 7. | Save the form as *MyControls*. | a. | Choose File→Save As. |

b. Type *MyControls*.

c. Click OK.

Align Controls

A form has a much more pleasing appearance when the controls in it are evenly aligned.

You can align controls by using the shortcut and Format menus.

* Select the controls you want to align and right-click on one of them. From the shortcut menu, select Align. You can then choose to align the Left, Right, Top, Bottom, or To Grid.

* To even out horizontal or vertical spacing of controls, select the controls and choose Format→Horizontal Spacing or Format→Vertical Spacing. You can choose to adjust the spacing by selecting Make Equal, Increase, or Decrease.

ACTIVITY 6-5

Aligning Controls

Activity Time:

5 minutes

Scenario:

You know that a form looks much better to the user if the labels and controls are neatly aligned and spaced. It can be difficult to do this by eye, so you want to see if there's a better way.

What You Do	How You Do It
1. Align the right sides of the CustomerID, Phone, Address, and City labels.	a. Click on the horizontal ruler to select the CustomerID, Phone, Address, and City label controls.
	b. Right-click on one of the selected controls and choose Align→Right.
2. Align the labels and text boxes for the phone and fax information, so the bottoms of the controls are even.	a. Use the vertical ruler or the lasso technique to select the Phone and Fax labels and text boxes.
	b. Display the shortcut menu and choose Align→Bottom.

3. Make the spacing of the City, Region, Country, and PostalCode labels and text boxes equal.

a. Select the City, Region, Country, and PostalCode labels and text boxes.

b. Choose Format→Horizontal Spacing→ Make Equal.

4. **View the form** to see if you're happy with the results. **Then close the form, saving the revisions.**

a. Click Form View.

b. Click the Close button.

c. Click Yes.

Move Controls

When you select a text box control in a form, Access assumes that you might also want to move the associated label control (and vice versa). In order to move just the control or controls you want, you need to watch for the correct mouse pointer to be displayed.

In the following graphic, the text box control for the Phone field is selected, but the associated label control also displays a move handle. If you want to move just the text box and not the label, the mouse pointer should look like a hand with a pointing finger as in the graphic. This will occur if you point to the move handle of the control you want to move.

If you want to move both the Phone text box and label controls, the mouse pointer should look like an open hand as shown in the following graphic. This will occur if you point to one of the edges of the selected control.

ACTIVITY 6-6

Moving Controls

Activity Time:
10 minutes

Scenario:
Sometimes you would like to be able to place a control manually. To do that, you need to know how to move the controls or controls you want to place.

What You Do	How You Do It
1. Open the MoveControls form in Design view and move the CustomerName text box closer to its label.	a. In the Database window, **right-click on MoveControls and choose Design view.** b. **Select the CustomerName text box.** c. **Place the mouse pointer over the move handle in the upper-left corner of the text box until it becomes a hand with a pointing finger.** d. **Click and drag the text box to the left** to place it closer to the CustomerName label.
2. Move the CustomerID label and text box to the upper-left corner of the form.	a. **Click on the CustomerID text box.** b. **Place the mouse pointer over the top or bottom edge of the text box until it becomes an open hand.** c. **Click and drag the label and the text box to the upper-left corner of the form.**
3. Move the Fax label closer to the Fax text box.	a. **Click on the Fax label.** b. **Place the mouse pointer over the move handle in the upper-left corner of the label until it becomes a hand with a pointing finger.** c. **Click and drag it closer to the Fax text box.**

4. Move all of the labels and text boxes containing address information lower on the form.	a. Use the ruler or lasso technique to select all of the labels and text boxes containing address information.
	b. Place the mouse pointer over all of the selected controls until it becomes an open hand.
	c. Click and drag the controls down on the form.
5. Close the form without saving changes to the design.	a. Click the Close button.
	b. Click No.

Modify the Design of the Form

You work in a form's Design view to make changes to the look and functionality of the form. The types of changes you may want to make include:

- Move, size, and align controls.

- Apply formatting to text boxes or labels.

- Add a title or other descriptive text.

- Change the size of the form.

Sizing a Form

To have a form display the way you want in Form view, work in Design view and coordinate the size of the window containing the form and the size of the form itself. You can size each horizontal section of the form and the width of the form. Trial and error will get the result you want.

ACTIVITY 6-7

Modifying the Design of a Form

Scenario:

You've created a form with the wizard and it looks like Figure 6-1. You decide that you would like the form to look more like Figure 6-2. So you're going to work in Design view to change the appearance.

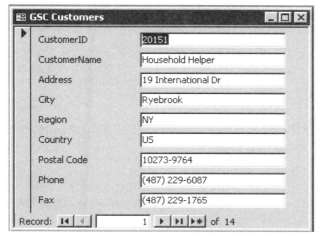

Figure 6-1: *The GSCCustomers form.*

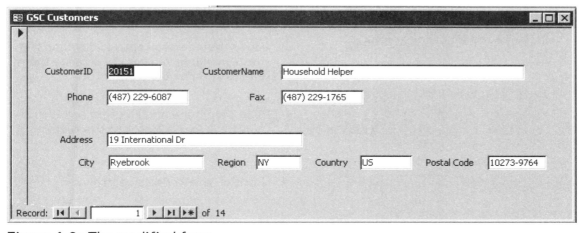

Figure 6-2: *The modified form.*

What You Do	How You Do It
1. **Open the GSCCustomers form in Design view and size the form window and form** to give you ample room to work.	a. In the Database window, **right-click on GSCCustomers and choose Design view.**
	b. **Place the mouse pointer over the lower-right corner of the form window until it becomes an angled double-headed arrow.**
	c. **Click and drag down and to the right** to enlarge the window.
	d. **Place the mouse pointer over the right edge of the form until it becomes a vertical line with a horizontal double-headed arrow.**
	e. **Click and drag the edge of the form to the right.**
	f. **Place the mouse pointer over the bottom edge of the form and drag the edge down.**
2. Using selection, moving, sizing, and alignment techniques, **arrange the controls on the form so that it is similar to the following graphic.**	a. **Move the customer name controls up next to the CustomerID controls.**
	b. **Move the Address controls down on the form so you have room to arrange the Phone and Fax controls.**
	c. **Size the Phone and Fax text boxes and move the labels closer to the text boxes.**
	d. **Position the Address controls.**
	e. **Align the controls as shown in the following graphic.**

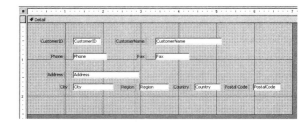

3. View the form to check the size of the window and the form. If necessary, make adjustments.

   a. **Click Form View.**

   b. If you want to make adjustments to the size of the window or the form, **click Design View.**

   c. **Size the window or the form.**

4. Now that you've made these changes to your form, you should **switch to Form View and check the tab order.**

   a. **Click Form View.**

   b. **Press the [Tab] key several times** to move from the first field in the form to the last. The Phone field would logically follow the CustomerName field in the form's new layout, but the tab order is based on the original layout.

5. **Return to Design View and correct the tab order.**

   a. **Click Design View.**

   b. **Choose View→Tab Order.**

   c. In the Tab Order dialog box, **click Auto Order, and then click OK.**

6. **Return to Form View and check the tab order.**

   a. **Click Form View.**

   b. **Click the [Tab] key** to move through the fields. The tab order has been corrected to better suit the form's new layout.

7. When you're satisfied with your design, **save the form as *MyGSCCustomers* and close the form.**

   a. **Choose File→Save As.**

   b. **Type*MyGSCCustomers*.**

   c. **Click OK.**

   d. **Click the Close button.**

TOPIC D

Use Forms to Work with Data

Now that you've learned some techniques for creating forms and customizing them, you will use forms to work with data.

Because forms can be customized and offer a more usable view of data, people who work with databases most commonly use forms to view and maintain their data. You need to know how to correctly select records and, because using forms to work with data in related tables has some special considerations, you need to know how to approach editing that data.

Use Forms to Work with Data

Most Access users work with their data by using forms. The techniques for editing values and records are the same as for working in Datasheet view.

- To find a record, click in the text box for the field on which you want to search and click the Find button.

- To delete a record, click the record selector and press [Delete], or click the Delete Record button.

- To add a record, click the New Record button on the navigation bar. A blank form is displayed for data entry.

- To delete a value, select the value and press [Delete].

- To edit a value, select the portion you wish to change and type the new value.

Edit Related Data

When you have referential integrity established between two tables (usually with a one-to-many relationship), you cannot delete a record on the one side of the relationship if related records exist on the many side. You also cannot change the value in the primary key field if matching values exist in the related foreign key field. These restrictions may affect the order in which you need to make changes to your data.

ACTIVITY 6-8

Using a Form to Edit Related Data

Scenario:

You have some routine data maintenance to do and plan to use forms you created because they make viewing the data easier. You need to delete a customer record. You also need to update your computer inventory data to reflect the fact that a person has left the company and his or her computer has been reassigned to someone else, and you need to add a record for a new computer.

What You Do	How You Do It
1. **Open the Customers form and view the record for The Value Store.**	a. In the Database window, **double-click on Customers.**
	b. **Click in the CustomerName field.**
	c. **Click the Find button.**
	d. In the Find What text box, **type** *The Value Store.*
	e. **Click Find Next.**
	f. **Click Cancel.**
2. **Notice the record selector at the left of the window.** It is the full height of the record and has the triangle icon indicating the current record.	
3. **Delete the record for The Value Store and close the form.**	a. **Click the record selector.**
	b. **Press [Delete] or click the Delete Record button** ⋈ **.**
	c. **Click Yes to delete the record.**
	d. **Close the form.**

4. **Open the Inventory form and view the record for Andrea Brown.** She has left the company and her computer has been reassigned to Josh Caldwell. **Attempt to delete her record.**

   a. **Open the Inventory form.**

   b. Using the Find button, **locate the Brown record.**

   c. Notice that there is a record selector for the employee record and record selectors for the computer records. **Click the record selector for the employee information.**

   d. **Press [Delete].**

5. **Observe the Microsoft Access message.** When you enforce referential integrity between tables, you are unable to delete a record if there is a related record in the other table.

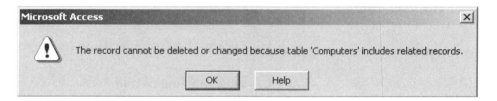

   Click Help and read about this error. You could delete the record about the computer and then delete Andrea Brown's record. But that would mean you would have to make a note of the computer data and then retype it. You'll try a more efficient way.

6. **Close Help and the message dialog box.**

   a. **Close the Help window.**

   b. **Click OK.**

7. **Notice that the computer record includes the EmployeeID field.** This is the field that links the information in the two tables. The most efficient way to edit this data is to first reassign the computer to Josh Caldwell by entering his ID. Then you'll be able to delete the record for Andrea Brown because there will be no related records.

8. Find the EmployeeID for Josh Caldwell and then enter that value in the EmployeeID field for the record for the computer with AssetTag 1052. Save the revised records.

   a. Click in the LastName field.

   b. Find the Caldwell record.

   c. Make a note of the EmployeeID: _____.

   d. Find the Brown record.

   e. In the EmployeeID field, **enter the EmployeeID for Josh Caldwell for the computer with AssetTag 1052.**

   f. Save the record.

9. Delete the record for Andrea Brown.

   a. Select the record.

   b. Press [Delete].

   c. Click Yes.

10. Edit the record for Edward Bernstein to assign him a new computer with the following data:

AssetTag: 1251

ManufacturerID: 3

DateReceived: (today's date)

PurchasePrice: $1,300

Warranty: Yes

Close the form.

   a. Find the Bernstein record.

   b. Click in the AssetTag field.

   c. Type *1251*.

   d. Press [Enter] or [Tab].

   e. Enter the remaining data:

     ManufacturerID: 3

     DateReceived: (today's date)

     PurchasePrice: $1,300

     Warranty: Yes

   f. Close the form.

Lesson 6 Follow-up

Your databases will likely contain vast amounts of data. To make viewing and maintaining this data easier, you'll want to create forms. You can create instant forms with the AutoForm feature, slightly more customized forms with the Form Wizard, and forms tailored to your specifications can be created in Design view. Once you have your forms in place, you can use them to sort and edit your data.

1. **When would you use the AutoForm feature to create your form instead of using the Form Wizard? What about the reverse?**

2. **What types of forms will you be creating for working with your data?**

LESSON 7
Creating and Using Reports

Lesson Time
55 minutes

Lesson Objectives:

In this lesson, you will create and modify reports to select, organize, and print data.

You will:

- Determine when to print a datasheet and when to create an AutoReport.
- Use the Report Wizard to create a report with groups of information.
- Compare the design of a report to the printed output.
- Create a calculated field in a report.
- Change the format of a control to affect its printed form.
- Use AutoFormat to change the overall look of a report.
- Adjust settings to eliminate blank pages in a report.

Introduction

Although you can print datasheets in Access, creating reports enables you to present your data in a more meaningful and professional-looking way. In this lesson, you'll learn how to create reports, include calculations in reports, and modify the design of reports.

Our work is often judged by the output we produce, and Access reports are the output from all the work you do to maintain important data. A professional-looking report that contains meaningful information is how you can demonstrate the importance and effectiveness of your database.

TOPIC A

Create an AutoReport

You've seen how fast an AutoForm can be created so, in this topic, you'll try out the AutoReport feature.

It seems everyone wants everything in a hurry. So, if your manager asks for a report and needs it right away, you may be able to use an AutoReport.

Create an AutoReport

Procedure Reference: Create an AutoReport

To create an AutoReport:

1. In the Database window, select the table or query on which you want to base the report.

2. On the toolbar, open the New Object drop-down list and choose AutoReport.

Data Sources for Reports

Reports can be based on one or more tables or queries.

Print Preview

If you want to see how a datasheet, form, or report will look when printed, click the Print Preview button on the toolbar. In the Print Preview window, you can view one, two, or multiple pages, by clicking the appropriate buttons on the Print Preview toolbar. You can use the Zoom drop-down list, the Zoom button, or the magnifying glass mouse pointer to change the magnification of the preview.

ACTIVITY 7-1

Creating an AutoReport

Data Files:

- UseReports.mdb

Scenario:

Before you have to deal with an urgent request for printed output of your data, you've decided to compare the results of printing a datasheet with the results of an AutoReport so you'll know which to use when.

What You Do	How You Do It
1. Open the UseReports database and then open the Inventory query. Preview how the query will look in printed form. Preview it at a size that enables you to read the data and view both pages that would be printed.	a. Open the UseReports database.
	b. In the Database window, **display the list of queries.**
	c. Open the Inventory query.
	d. Click the Print Preview button .
	e. Place the mouse pointer over the preview until it becomes a magnifying glass.
	f. Click the mouse button to enlarge the preview to 100%.
	g. Use the scroll bars and navigation bar, as necessary, to view both pages.

2. What features does the printed datasheet have?

What disadvantages are there to printing the query datasheet?

3. Print the datasheet and then close the Preview and datasheet windows.	a. Click the Print button .
	b. On the Preview toolbar, **click Close.**
	c. Close the datasheet window.

4. Create an AutoReport for the Inventory query.

    a. Verify that the Inventory query is selected in the Database window.

    b. Open the New Object drop-down list and choose AutoReport.

---

5. Examine the preview of the AutoReport.

How does the AutoReport compare to the printed datasheet?

---

6. Close the preview window and save the report as *MyAutoReport*. If necessary, close the report Design window.

    a. On the Preview toolbar, click Close.

    b. Click Save.

    c. In the Report Name text box, type *MyAutoReport*.

    d. Click OK.

    e. Close the report Design window.

Topic B

Create a Report Using a Wizard

Now that you've seen what a printed datasheet and an AutoReport would look like, you're going to using a wizard to create a report with the same data.

If having a datasheet print with data split across pages or printing a multiple page AutoReport without a title, date, or, page numbers is not satisfactory, you'll have to turn to the Report Wizard to create a more customized report. Even if you go on later to modify the design of the report, starting with the wizard is always the most efficient.

Create a Report Using a Wizard

Procedure Reference: Create a Report Using the Report Wizard

To create a report using the Report Wizard:

1. In the Database window, in the Objects bar, select Reports.

2. Double-click on Create Report By Using Wizard.

3. Using the Tables/Queries drop-down list, select the data source for the report.

4. Move the fields you want included in the report from the Available Fields list to the Selected Fields list by using the arrow buttons.

5. Repeat steps 3 and 4 for any additional data sources.

6. Click Next.

7. If necessary, choose the grouping levels and grouping options you want and click Next.

8. Select the sort order for the detail records and click Next.

9. Select the layout for the report and click Next.

10. Select the style for the report and click Next.

11. Enter a title for the report and select whether you want the report displayed in Print Preview or Design view. Click Finish.

Order of Fields

When using the Report Wizard, the order in which fields appear in the Selected Fields list determines their left-to-right order in the report. The placement of the controls representing the fields can be changed in Design view.

Grouping and Sorting

When a group level is included in a report, the records are automatically sorted first by the values in the grouping field. Additional group levels are used as additional sorting levels. You determine the order of the detail records within a group by designating, in the Report Wizard, the fields on which they should be sorted. So, for example, if you've created a report to list employees by department name and have a group level of DepartmentName, the records will be grouped by that name and the department names will be arranged in alphabetical order. Then you should designate how you want the list of employees within a department sorted; it might be by an employee ID or by last name.

Report Title and Object Name

When you enter a title for a report, that entry will be printed at the top of the report and is also used as the name of the report object in the Database window. You can change the name of the report object in the Database window, or you can change the printed title by opening the report in Design view.

ACTIVITY 7-2

Creating a Report Using a Wizard

Scenario:

The Controller of the company has asked you for a report that lists, by department, the current computer inventory. You want to organize the information correctly and print it in a legible and professional-looking format like that in Figure 7-1.

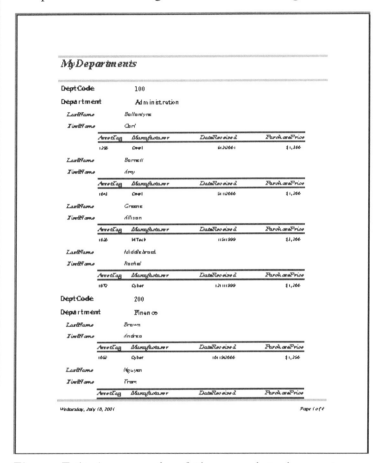

Figure 7-1: *An example of the completed report.*

What You Do	How You Do It
1. **Start the Report Wizard.**	a. In the Database window, **display Reports.**
	b. **Double-click on Create Report By Using Wizard.**

2. **Base the report on the Inventory query, include the following fields, and then continue with the wizard.**
   - DeptCode
   - Department
   - LastName
   - FirstName
   - AssetTag
   - Manufacturer
   - DateReceived
   - PurchasePrice

   a. Open the Tables/Queries drop-down list and select Query: Inventory.

   b. **Click the rightward-pointing double arrow to move all the available fields to the Selected Fields list.** Adding all fields and then removing the ones you don't want can sometimes be more efficient.

   c. In the Selected Fields list, **select ManufacturerID.**

   d. **Click the leftward-pointing single arrow.**

   e. **Remove the Warranty field from the Selected Fields list.**

   f. **Click Next.**

3. **Observe the report sample.** The wizard has grouped the data first by departments and then by employees. You could choose to group it in other ways.

4. **View the samples of the other possible groupings. Then view the additional information that is available.**

   a. In the list of views, **click By Employees and view the sample.**

   b. In the list of views, **click By Computers and view the sample.**

   c. In the list of views, **click By Manufacturers and view the sample.**

   d. **Click Show Me More Information.**

5. **Read the Report Wizard Tips.** The table relationships determine how the wizard can group the data. If none of the choices in the wizard met your needs, you could choose the fields yourself.

6. **Close the Report Wizard Tips.** The report request you received was to have the data by departments so **choose the appropriate organization for the data.**

   Continue with the wizard without adding any additional grouping levels.

   a. **Click Close.**

   b. In the list of views, **select By Departments.**

   c. **Click Next.**

   d. Since you don't need any additional levels of groups, **click Next.**

7. Sort the detail records in ascending order by the asset tag number, and then continue with the wizard.

   a. Open the drop-down list for the first sort order box.

   b. Choose AssetTag.

   c. Click Next.

8. View the samples of the various layouts, select the one you prefer (the example in Figure 7-1 uses Outline 1), and then continue with the wizard.

   a. In the Layout list, select each option and view the sample.

   b. Select Outline 1.

   c. Click Next.

9. View the samples of the various styles, select the one you prefer (the example in Figure 7-1 uses Corporate), and then continue with the wizard.

   a. In the list of styles, select each style and view the sample.

   b. Select Corporate.

   c. Click Next.

10. Enter a title of *MyDepartments* and then preview all pages of your report.

When previewing a report, you can use the Two Pages and Multiple Pages buttons to get a big picture look at the layout of your report.

   a. In the title text box, type *MyDepartments*.

   b. Verify that Preview The Report is selected.

   c. Click Finish.

   d. Use the scroll and navigation bars to view all the data and pages.

11. What are some of the features of the report?

12. Using the Close button for the Preview window, **close the window.**

a. In the Preview window, **click the Close
button.**

 If you click Close on the Print Preview
toolbar, Design view of the report will be
displayed. Close that window as well.

TOPIC C

Examine a Report in Design View

You've seen three different ways you can create reports, but it's unlikely that any of those
methods will always produce the exact result you need. To customize a report, you need to be
familiar with the report design environment and to be able to relate what you do there to the
report output. This topic will get you started.

For many database users, the ability to produce customized reports is second only to knowing
how to maintain the data. And to customize a report, you need to understand the design
environment.

Examine the Design of a Report

The arrangement of controls in report Design view determines how the data in a report will be
printed.

Report Sections

The design of a report is organized by sections and the placement of controls in a particular section determines how often the data or text in a control will print. For
example, information in the Report Header section will print once at the beginning of
the report. Information in the Page Footer section will print at the bottom of every
page. Controls in the Detail section will print for every record in the report.

The Property Sheet

In Access, everything is an object and almost all objects have properties associated
with them. In modifying the design of a report, you can use these properties to change
or enter settings that affect how the report will look. You access the properties by a
report object by selecting the object in Design view and clicking the Properties button;
this opens the property sheet containing all the associated properties.

ACTIVITY 7-3

Examining the Design of a Report

Scenario:

You know that you want to be able to customize reports so you've decided to spend a little time familiarizing yourself with how the report design determines the final format.

What You Do	How You Do It
1. Preview the DepartmentalInventory report, maximize the window if necessary, and view all pages. This is similar to the report you created using the wizard. **Then switch to Design view.**	a. In the Objects bar, **select Reports.** b. **Double-click on DepartmentalInventory.** c. **Maximize the preview window.** d. **Use the navigation bar to view all pages.** e. On the Print Preview toolbar, **click Close.** f. **Click Design View.**

2. Examine the structure of the report design.

   What information is in the Report Header and when does it print?

   Notice that each group you designated in the wizard—DeptCode and LastName—has a header section.

   What information is contained in the Detail section?

   And what about the page footer?

3. Use the property sheet to determine which controls on the report are labels and which are text boxes.

✒ You can move the property sheet by dragging it by the title bar.

a. On the Report Design toolbar, **click the Properties button** 🖼️ .

b. **Select the control containing the report title "Departmental Inventory."**

c. **Observe the title bar of the property sheet.** It indicates that the control is a label that has been named Title.

d. **Select other controls on the report and view the property sheet.**

---

4. **How could you characterize the contents of the types of controls found in this report?**

---

5. **Close the property sheet.**

a. In the Property Sheet dialog box, **click the Close button.**

TOPIC D

Create a Calculated Field

One of the many things you may want to do to customize a report is to include some type of calculation in the report. This topic will show you one example of that.

If the calculation you need is not part of the query on which you've based a report, you don't have to go back and revise the query. You can create the calculation right in the report design.

The Toolbox

You use the Toolbox (refer to Figure 7-2) to create new controls in the design of a report. The Select Objects and Control Wizards tools are selected in the Toolbox by default. The Select Objects tool enables you to click on controls in the report design to select them. The Control Wizards tool automatically runs a wizard if one is available for the control you are creating.

You can get additional information on each tool by selecting the tool and pressing [F1]. Press [Esc] to close the information pop-up box.

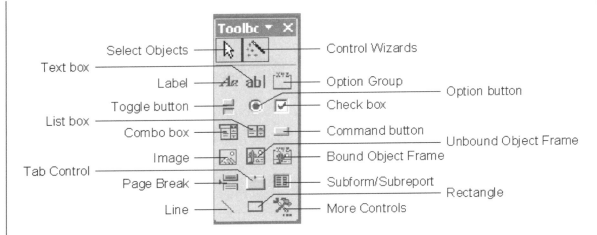

Figure 7-2: *The Toolbox.*

Create a Calculated Field

Procedure Reference: Create a Calculated Control

To create a calculated control on a report:

1. Open the report in Design view.

2. If necessary, display the Toolbox by clicking on the Toolbox button.

3. In the Toolbox, click on the Text Box tool.

4. Click (or drag) on the report design surface where you wish to place the calculated control.

5. If necessary, click in the text box control to place the insertion point.

6. Type an equal sign (=) and the formula for the calculation.

7. Press [Enter] or click away from the control.

Field Names and Brackets

When you type an expression, each field name must be enclosed in brackets.

Activity 7-4

Creating a Calculated Field

Scenario:

You've already created this report for the Controller using the Report Wizard. But now the Controller calls and tells you that he plans to amortize the cost of computers over three years and asks if you could include that calculation in the report. You say,"No problem!"

What You Do	How You Do It
1. Add a control containing a formula that will spread the cost of each computer listed in the report over a period of three years.	a. If necessary to display the Toolbox, on the Report Design toolbar, **click the Toolbox button** ✎ .
Note that, when you place the text box control, it contains the word Unbound. This is because you have not yet designated the contents of the control.	b. In the Toolbox, **click on the Text Box tool** `ab|` .
	c. **Click in the Detail section to the right of the PurchasePrice control** to add the control to the report.
	d. **Click in the text box control.**
	e. **Type =[PurchasePrice]/3.**

✎ The same techniques for selecting and moving controls used in the form design environment work in the report design environment. You can also move the Toolbox by dragging it by the title bar.

2. Delete the default label for the control. Add the heading *Amortized* to the right of the PurchasePrice heading. Close the Toolbox when you're done and preview the report.	a. **Click on the default label control** to select it.
	b. **Press [Delete].**
	c. In the Toolbox, **click on the Label tool** `Aa` .
	d. In the LastName Header section to the right of the PurchasePrice label, **drag to create the label control.**
	e. **Type** *Amortized.*
	f. In the Toolbox, **click the Close button.**
	g. **Click the Print Preview button.**

3. **Observe the report and the results of the calculation.**

Amortized

433.33333333333

Amortized

400

Amortized

1066.6666666667

Amortized

400

Are your calculation results correct? The format is probably not what you would want so you'll go on to change that.

---

4. Before you do any more work on the report, **save it as** *MyInventoryReport*.

   a. **Choose File→Save As.**

   b. **Type** *MyInventoryReport*.

   c. **Click OK.**

   d. On the Print Preview toolbar, **click Close.**

TOPIC E

Change the Format of a Control

Now that you know how to add controls to a report, you'll learn how to use properties so that the contents of controls will print just the way you want.

Imagine that you're going to print a report for distribution at an important meeting and you want to make the very best impression. Data is more useful as information when it's formatted in a way that best conveys its meaning.

Change the Format of a Control

Procedure Reference: Change the Format of a Control

To change the format of a control in a report:

1. Open the report in Design view.

2. Select the control and click the Properties button or right-click on the control and choose Properties.

3. If necessary, select the Format tab in the property sheet.

4. In the Format property box, open the drop-down list and choose the format you want.

5. Close the property sheet.

6. Preview the report to see the new format.

The Now() Function

Access has many built-in functions. The Now() function returns the current date and time according to your computer's system clock.

ACTIVITY 7-5

Changing the Format of a Control

Setup:

MyInventoryReport is open in Design view.

Scenario:

You've created the calculation you need on the report. Now all you need to do is format it as currency. You've also decided you would like to have the report date print in a different format. You'll preview the report to check your results.

What You Do	How You Do It
1. Change the format of the new calculated control so it will print the values it contains in Currency format.	a. In the Detail section, **select the control containing the formula you entered.**
	b. On the Report Design toolbar, **click the Properties button.**
	c. **Click in the Format property box.**
	d. **Display the drop-down list and choose Currency.**
	e. **Click Print Preview.**
2. **Notice the format of the report date in the report header.** Right now, it's set to the following format. *Wednesday, July 18, 2001*	
3. Change the date format to 01/01/2001 and preview the report.	a. **Switch to Design view.**
	b. In the Report Header section, **select the control containing the Now() function.**
	c. **Open the Format property drop-down list and choose Short Date.**
	d. **Click Print Preview.**

4. **Save the report.** If you'd like to make changes to the format property of other controls, now is your opportunity. **Save the report when you're happy with the results.**

a. **Switch to Design view.**

b. **Click Save.**

c. To change properties of any control, **select the control and select the property setting you want.**

d. **Preview the report** to see the effect of any changes.

e. **Return to Design view and save the report.**

TOPIC F
Change the Style of a Report

You've seen how you can choose a report style as part of creating a report with the wizard. But what if you change your mind? Do you have to start all over? In this topic, you'll use a feature available in report Design view that enables to you change the style.

You can spend an enormous amount of time fine-tuning the look of a report. Instead, to give it a fresh face quickly, you can use the AutoFormat feature.

Change the Style of a Report

Procedure Reference: Change the Style of a Report

To change the style of a report:

1. Open the report in Design view.

2. Choose Edit→Select Report, or click the Report Selector.

3. On the Report Design toolbar, click the AutoFormat button.

4. In the Report AutoFormats list, select the new format.

5. Click OK.

6. Preview the report to see the new style.

ACTIVITY 7-6

Changing the Format of a Report

Setup:

MyInventoryReport is open in Design view.

Scenario:

You've done a little work in the report design environment, but imagine that you're just not happy with the overall appearance of your report. You could try adjusting a number of properties, you could start all over with the Report Wizard, or the AutoFormat feature might do the work for you.

What You Do	How You Do It
1. Close the property sheet. Select the report and open the AutoFormat dialog box. Choose a report format you like based on its preview in the dialog box. Apply that format and preview the report.	a. In the Property Sheet dialog box, **click the Close button.** b. Choose Edit→Select Report or click the Report Selector. 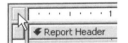 c. On the Report Design toolbar, **click the AutoFormat button** . d. In the Report AutoFormats list, **select a format and observe the preview.** e. **Preview each of the formats and select the one you prefer.** f. **Click OK.** g. **Print preview your report.**
2. If you're happy with the appearance of the report, **save and close it.** Otherwise, apply a different AutoFormat. Save the report when you're done.	a. **Switch to Design view.** b. **Click Save.** c. **Click the Close button.**

TOPIC G

Adjust Report Width

Getting the width of your report in Design view in synch with margin settings and page width seems like it should be easy, but it's something Access report designers often overlook. This topic will show you your options and the often-used quick fix.

If report width, margins, and paper size aren't set properly, your report may print with every other page being nearly blank. This wastes paper and causes the page numbers in your report to be wrong. This topic will show you the cause and the cure.

Adjust Report Width

Procedure Reference: Adjust the Report Width and Margins

To quickly adjust the report width and margins to appropriate settings for the paper size so the report doesn't have some nearly blank pages:

1. Open the report in Design view.

2. On the horizontal ruler, note the width of the report.

3. Calculate left and right margin settings that, when added to the report width, are no greater than the width of the paper.

4. Choose File→Page Setup and enter the Left and Right margin values.

5. Click OK.

6. Preview the report to check your results.

Default Margin Settings

The default margin settings for an Access report are 1 inch at the top and bottom and the left and right sides.

ACTIVITY 7-7

Adjusting Report Width

Scenario:
You've spent a lot of time perfecting your report and merrily sent it off to the printer. But, when you picked it up, you saw that every other page is mostly blank. Now you need to fix it—and fast!

What You Do	How You Do It
1. **Print Preview FinalReport viewing two pages side by side.**	a. In the Database window, **right-click on FinalReport and choose Print Preview.**
	b. On the Print Preview toolbar, **click the Two Pages button** .
2. **Observe the report.** The second page is mostly blank; the lines around the report title spill over to the second page.	
3. **Preview the rest of the report.**	a. On the Print Preview toolbar, **click the Multiple Pages button** .
	b. **Drag to select 2 X 3 Pages.**
4. **Observe the report.** Every other page is blank; it appears that the line in the report footer may also be too wide.	
5. **Switch to Design view and note the width of the report. Open the Page Setup dialog box and notice the margin settings.**	a. On the Print Preview toolbar, **click the Design view button.**
	b. On the horizontal ruler, **note the width of the report.** It is approximately 6.75 inches wide.
	c. **Choose File→Page Setup and note the margin settings.** Each margin is set to 1 inch.

6. Why are these settings causing the blank pages?

What do you think your options might be for fixing this problem?

---

7. Change the margins to eliminate the blank pages and preview the report. Save and close the report when you've eliminated all blank pages.

   a. In the Page Setup dialog box, **change the Left and Right margin values to 0.75.**

   b. **Click OK.**

   c. **Print Preview all pages of the report.** The blank pages have been removed.

   d. **Close Print Preview.**

   e. **Click Save.**

   f. **Click the Close button.**

---

8. Close the UseReports database and close Access.

   a. In the Database window, **click the Close button.**

   b. In the Microsoft Access window, **click the Close button.**

Lesson 7 Follow-up

Looking to present your data in a professional and meaningful way? Then you'll want to create a report. As you have seen, you can create a report instantly with the AutoReport function, while slightly more customized reports can be built with the Report Wizard. For even more customization options, you'll turn to Design view. To add functionality to your report, you can create a calculated field controls, and to modify the look of your report, you can use the AutoFormat feature or adjust layout options such as margin size.

1. What kinds of reports will you be creating for your data?

2. What uses can you think of for calculated fields in your reports?

Follow-up

In this course, you have learned the basic skills you need in order to begin designing and creating relational databases with Access. Now you can go out and build databases that will harness the power of your company's information. You can run queries to find information on the spot and turn raw data into useful, customized forms and reports that will help your business to run more smoothly.

What's Next?

Access 2002: Level 2 is the next course in this series. There is also a Level 3 course available.

APPENDIX A

Microsoft Office Specialist Program

Selected Element K courseware addresses Microsoft Office Specialist skills. The following tables indicate where Access 2002 skills are covered. For example, 1-3 indicates the lesson and activity number applicable to that skill.

Core Skill Sets and Skills Being Measured	Access 2002: Level 1	Access 2002: Level 2	Access 2002: Level 3	Access 2002: Level 4
Creating and Using Databases				
Create Access databases	1-5			
Open database objects in multiple views	3-3, 5-1, 6-7, 7-2			
Move among records	4-2			
Format datasheets	4-2			
Creating and Modifying Tables				
Create and modify tables	3-2, 4-1			
Add a pre-defined input mask to a field		2-3		
Create lookup fields		2-5		
Modify field properties	4-1	2-3		
Creating and Modifying Queries				
Create and modify Select queries	5-2			
Add calculated fields to Select queries	5-6			
Creating and Modifying Forms				
Create and display forms	6-1, 6-2			
Modify form properties	6-3, 6-7			
Viewing and Organizing Information				

APPENDIX A

Core Skill Sets and Skills Being Measured	Access 2002: Level 1	Access 2002: Level 2	Access 2002: Level 3	Access 2002: Level 4
Enter, edit, and delete records	4-1, 5-5, 6-8	5-3		
Create queries	5-2		2-2	
Sort records	5-3			
Filter records		3-1		
Defining Relationships				
Create one-to-many relationships	3-7, 3-8			
Enforce referential integrity	3-7, 3-8			
Producing Reports				
Create and format reports	7-2			
Add calculated controls to reports	7-4			
Preview and print reports	7-1, 7-7			
Integrating with Other Applications				
Import data to Access		1-1		
Export data from Access		1-3		
Create a simple data access page		7-1		

Expert Skill Sets And Skills Being Measured	Access 2002: Level 1	Access 2002: Level 2	Access 2002: Level 3	Access 2002: Level 4
Creating and Modifying Tables				
Use data validation		2-1, 2-2		
Link tables				4-1
Create lookup fields and modify lookup field properties		2-6		
Create and input masks		2-4		
Creating and Modifying Forms				
Create a form in design view			5-2, 5-3	
Create a switchboard and set startup options				1-1, 1-2, 1-3, 1-4, 1-5
Add subform controls to access forms		5-5		
Refining Queries				
Specify multiple query criteria	5-4			
Create and apply advanced filters		3-2		

Expert Skill Sets And Skills Being Measured	Access 2002: Level 1	Access 2002: Level 2	Access 2002: Level 3	Access 2002: Level 4
Create and run parameter queries		4-2, 4-3		
Create and run action queries		4-5, 4-6		
Use aggregate functions in queries	5-8			
Producing Reports				
Create and modify reports			6-3	
Add subreport controls to access reports		6-5		
Sort and group data in reports		6-1		
Defining Relationships				
Establish one-to-many relationships	3-7, 3-8		1-2	
Establish many-to-many relationships	3-7, 3-8		1-3, 1-4	
Operating Access on the Web				
Create and modify a data access page		7-2		2-1, 2-2, 2-3, 2-4
Save pivottables and pivotcharts views to data access pages			2-3, 2-4, 2-5	2-5, 2-6, 2-7
Using Access Tools				
Import xml documents into access				4-4
Export access data to xml documents				4-5
Encrypt and decrypt databases				3-9
Compact and repair databases			1-5	
Assign database security				3-3, 3-7, 3-8
Replicate a database				4-6
Creating Database Applications				
Create access modules				5-1, 5-2, 5-3, 5-4, 5-5, 5-6, 5-7
Use the database splitter				3-1, 3-2, 3-3, 3-4
Create an MDE file				3-10

NOTES

LESSON LABS

Due to classroom setup constraints, some labs cannot be keyed in sequence immediately following their associated lesson. Your instructor will tell you whether your labs can be practiced immediately following the lesson or whether they require separate setup from the main lesson content.

LESSON 1 LAB 1

Creating and Exploring a New Database

Data Files:

* Solution MyOrderEntry

Scenario:

Your manager needs you to create an order entry database to store customer information, order information, order details, payment information and product information. You decide to create the database based on the Order Entry database template. Name the database file "MyOrderEntry" and save it in the My Documents folder.

 The Solution MyOrderEntry file is a completed file of this activity. You can compare your results to this file.

1.	In Access, **create a new database based on the Order Entry template.**
2.	**Name the database file *MyOrderEntry* and save it in the My Documents folder.**
3.	**Accept the default list of tables and fields.**
4.	**Select the screen display style of your choice; and then select the report style of your choice.**
5.	**Accept the title of "Order Entry" and finish the wizard.**
6.	**Close the company information form (or enter information, if you like).**

7. Next, take a look to see what you've got to work with. In the Order Entry database, **open the form that enables you to enter/view orders by customer and view the fields. Close the form and open the form to enter/view other information.**

8. Use the Form Switchboard to **open the various data entry forms. View the fields on each form.**

9. Return to the Main Switchboard and see what the Preview Reports option provides.

10. **Return to the Main Switchboard and exit this database.**

LESSON 2 LAB 1

Planning an Access Database

Scenario:

You are responsible for designing your company's Human Resources database to track employees and their related information, including personal data, department, pay rate, benefits, and parking lot assignment. Based on a set of fields you've decided upon, you need to create a design diagram that prepares you to create the database.

1. You've decided you need to include the following fields in the Human Resources database: EmployeeID, FirstName, LastName, Address, City, State, Zip, Phone, HireDate, Hours, PayRate, ParkingLotCode, ParkingLotName, ParkingFee, Health, DepartmentCode, DepartmentName, and Comments. Using this field list and following the guidelines on naming fields and tables, **draw a diagram of the tables you'll need with the fields that each will contain.** You can compare your diagram to Figure 2-A.

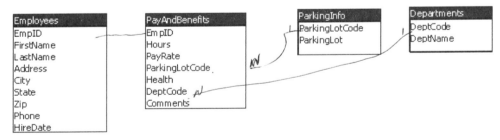

Figure 2-A: *Deciding on tables.*

2. **Designate fields to be used as the primary key field for each table. Mark the primary key fields with a "P." Mark the foreign key fields with an "F." Does your diagram resemble Figure 2-B?**

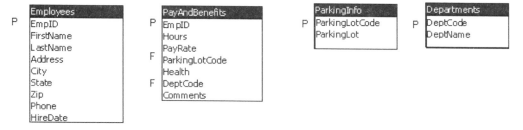

Figure 2-B: *Designating primary and foreign keys.*

3. **Finalize your design diagram by indicating the type of relationship that exists between the data in the related tables. Identify each relationship by drawing a line from the primary key field in one table to the foreign key field in each related table. Mark each end of the line with a "1" or an "N," as appropriate. You can compare your completed diagram to Figure 2-C.**

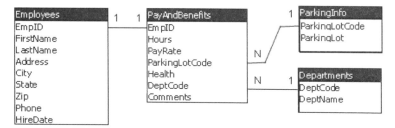

Figure 2-C: *Identifying the database relationships.*

LESSON 3 LAB 1

Creating a Database and Adding Tables

Data Files:

- Solution MyCustomers

Scenario:

Your manager has asked you to create a database for storing information about customers and their orders, as depicted in the following graphic. Create a new blank database called "MyCustomers" and, within that database, create three tables: Customers, Orders, and Billing. You can use the Table Wizard to create the first two tables, and then create the Billing table in Design view.

 The Solution MyCustomers file is a completed file of this activity. You can compare your results to this file.

---

1. **Create and save a new blank Access MDB file. Name the new database** *MyCustomers* **and save it in the My Documents folder.**

---

2. **Use the Table Wizard to create the Customers table.** From the Sample Tables list, **select Customers and include the following fields:**
   - CustomerID
   - CompanyName
   - BillingAddress
   - City
   - StateOrProvince
   - PostalCode
   - PhoneNumber
   - FaxNumber

   Accept the default name and let the wizard choose the primary key field for you. After viewing the new table, **close it.**

---

3. **Use the Table Wizard to create and save the Orders table.** From the Sample Tables list, **select the Orders table and the Order Details table to include the following fields:**

   - From the Orders table, OrderID
   - From the Orders table, OrderDate
   - From the OrderDetails table, ProductID
   - From the OrderDetails table, Quantity
   - From the Orders table, CustomerID

   Accept the default name and let the wizard choose the primary key field for you. Accept the relationship created by the wizard.

4. **Use Design view to create and save the Billing table with the following specifications:**

   - A CustomerID field with a data type of AutoNumber.
   - A FirstOrder field with a data type of Date/Time and a format of Short Date.
   - A ContactLastName field with a data type of Text.
   - A ContactFirstName field with a data type of Text.
   - An Account Number field with a data type of Text and a field size of 14.

   Set the CustomerID field as the primary key field. Save the table as *Billing* **and close it.**

5. **Establish the appropriate relationships between the tables. Enforce referential integrity between them.**

6. **Close the MyCustomers database.**

LESSON 4 LAB 1

Working with the Design and Data for Tables

Data Files:

- Campbiz.mdb
- Solution CampBiz

Scenario:

Imagine that you run a specialty camping business that makes tents, sleeping bags, backpacks, and other accessories. In your company database, you use the Customers table to keep track of people you do business with. You need to add a new customer to the Customer table and you need to update the details of another customer. To make the database more efficient, you also want to add some inventory numbers and remove redundant data, as well as make some slight changes to the design of the Products and Orders table. In browsing the Categories information, investigate to see how a subdatasheet can be useful for viewing related records.

 The Solution CampBiz file is a completed file of this activity. You can compare your results to this file.

---

1. In the CampBiz database, **enter the following record in the Customers table:**
   - CustomerNum: *300*
   - CustomerName: *Maple River Outfitters*
   - ContactLName: *Sharp*
   - ContactFName: *Todd*
   - Street: *5 Forrest Way*
   - City: *Hamlin*
   - State: *MN*
   - PostalCode: *56789*

---

2. In the Customers table, **sort the records by the State column and then by the CustomerName column.**

---

3. The contact person at Tent City has changed. **Locate the record of the customer named "Tent City."** In Edit mode, **change the name of the contact to** *Steve Clark.* **Close the table and save the changes.**

---

4. In Design view of the Orders table, **perform the following modifications, save the changes to the design of the table and, before closing the table, switch to Datasheet view to see the results.**

   - Change the field name for Rep to *RepID*.
   - Change the field name for Day to *Date*.
   - Rearrange the order of the fields, so that the RepID field is after the CustomerNum field.
   - Change the properties of the Date field so that it displays the date in Short Date format.

5. In Design view of the Products table, **perform the following modifications, save the changes to the design of the table, and, before closing the table, switch to Datasheet view to see the results.**

   - Above the CategoryID field, insert a new field for the UnitsInStock. Set the data type to Number.
   - Above the CategoryID field, insert a new field for the UnitsOnOrder. Set the data type to Number.
   - Delete the CategoryName field and the data that it contains.

6. **Open the Categories table. Open the subdatasheet for one of the records. Complete the following sentence:** The related records, displayed in the subdatasheet, are drawn from the _____ table. **Close the subdatasheet and the Categories table.**

7. **Close the CampBiz database.**

LESSON 5 LAB 1

Creating and Modifying the Design of Select Queries

Data Files:

- BookBiz.mdb
- Solution BookBiz

Scenario:

Imagine that you run a book bindery business. Your database includes tables that store information about each book, each order placed, and customers. In this activity, you will create several queries to answer business-related questions, such as the following:

   - Which books have sold?
   - Which book orders have been for 250 or more books?
   - How many sales transactions were recorded by the sales rep whose ID is EN1-22?
   - Which transactions did sales rep EN1-22 have on August 16, 2001?
   - How much did each individual book order cost?

LESSON LABS

1. **Open the BookBiz database.**

2. Imagine that you would like to see a listing of which books have sold. **Use the Query Wizard to display data from both the BookOrders and Books tables.** From the BookOrders table, **add the SalesID, Date, and Quantity fields.** From the Books table, **add the BookNumber and BookPrice fields. Indicate that you want to see the Detail records. Give your query the title of** *MyBookSales*.

3. Next, suppose you want to view only a portion of the records. First, you want to view all of the orders that were a quantity of 250 or greater. **Use criteria to select just the records you want. Record the number of records that satisfy this criteria: _____.**

   You want to view all the records for the sales rep whose ID number is EN1-22. **Enter the appropriate criteria. Record the number of records that satisfy this criteria: _____.**

   Next, you want to know how many of the sales records for sales rep EN1-22 occurred on 8/16/2001. **Enter the appropriate criteria. Record the number of records that satisfy this criteria: _____.**

   Save your revised query as *MySelectBookSales* **and close it.**

4. Next, you'll create a query that answers the question: "How much did each individual book order cost?" **Create a query in Design view that includes the BookOrders table and the Customers table. Add the CustomerName, Quantity, and BookNumber fields to the design grid. Sort the query records by CustomerName. Run the query and view the results.**

5. **Return to the query's Design view and add the Books table to the query.** From the Books table, **add the Title field to the design grid.**

6. **Create a field that calculates the total price each customer owes for each book order. (Multiply the Quantity field from the BookOrders table by the BookPrice field from the Books table.) Change the default calculated field name to** *OrderCost*. **Run the query and, before closing it, save it as** *MyBookCosts*.

7. **Close the BookBiz database.**

LESSON 6 LAB 1

Creating and Modifying Forms

Data Files:

- BreadBiz.mdb

- Solution BreadBiz

Scenario:

Imagine that you run a company that supplies bread mixes to gourmet and specialty shops. You want to create a data entry form that will make it easier to add new customers and refer to customer orders. You'll need to include customer information, as well as order details. Use the Form Wizard to quickly create a basic form and then modify the form you created.

 The Solution BreadBiz file is a completed file of this activity. You can compare your results to this file.

1. **Open the BreadBiz database.**

2. **Use the Form Wizard to create a form based on the Customers and OrderDetails tables.** From the Customers table, **add all the fields to the selected field list.** From the OrderDetails table, **add all the fields to the selected fields list.**

3. **Specify that you want to view the information in the form by Customers.**

4. **Use the Datasheet layout. Choose a form style you like. Save the form as** *MyCustomers*. **Save the subform as** *MyOrderDetails Subform*.

5. **Customize the appearance of the form by selecting, sizing, aligning, and moving controls, so that it resembles the following figure (Figure 6-A).**

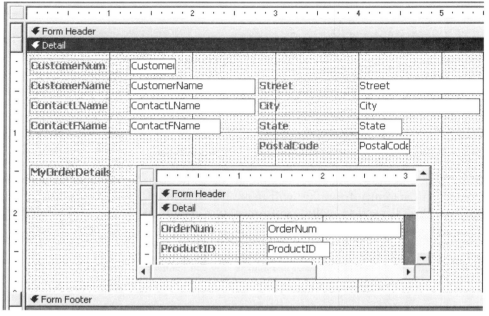

Figure 6-A: *The revised MyCustomers form.*

6. **Save the modified form design and view the form.**

7. **Close the form and close the BreadBiz database.**

LESSON 7 LAB 1

Creating and Modifying Reports

Data Files:

- PersonnelBiz.mdb

- Solution PersonnelBiz

Scenario:

The PersonnelBiz database contains basic data about employees, compensation, departments, and parking lots. You want to compile some of this data into various reports. You will use the Report Wizard to create a phone list report based on a query. You will also work in Design view to make some modifications to a report that focuses on the employee payroll .

✎ The Solution PersonnelBiz file is a completed file of this activity. You can compare your results to this file.

1. **Open the PersonnelBiz database.**

2. In the upcoming days, the company parking lots are being re-paved and you'll need to notify employees by calling them as necessary. **Use the Report Wizard to create a printed phone list report based on the ParkingLot query.**
   - Add the following fields: FirstName, LastName, ParkingLot, and Phone.
   - View your data by Employees.
   - Group the report based on the ParkingLot.
   - Sort by the FirstName field.
   - Select the Stepped layout and Corporate style for the report.
   - Name the report: *MyPhoneList*.
   - Preview the report.

   Close the report.

3. Suppose you already created another report and want to complete it by enhancing its appearance and including an annual salary figure. **Open the EmployeePay report.**

4. In Design view, **apply the Soft Gray AutoFormat** to change the look of the report.

5. You want to add a field that calculates the annual salary. Under the Annual Salary label control, **create a field that multiplies Weekly Hours, Hourly Pay Rate, and 52. Delete the default label for the control and align the text box control as necessary. Change the format of the new calculated control so that it prints the values in Currency format with zero decimal places. Delete the default label for the control and align the text box control as necessary.**

6. **Change the format of the text control in the Page Footer section that contains the Date function from Short Date to Long Date.**

7. **Save the revised report as *MyEmployeePay*.**

NOTES

SOLUTIONS

Lesson 1

Activity 1-1

1. What are some examples of sets of data that you use in your personal life?

    Answers may include a cookbook, a TV program guide, mail-order catalogs, and a household inventory.

2. What are some examples of collections of data you use in your job?

    Answers may include personnel records, customer or vendor lists, and purchasing information.

3. What are some other examples of collections of data that you encounter daily?

    Answers may include real estate listings, health records, some Web sites, bank records, and information gathered by scanners at a grocery store.

Activity 1-2

1. <u>False</u>   The VP of Finance needs to analyze potential profits for a new product line.

2. <u>True</u>   The Customer Service manager wants to be able to handle customer orders and invoices electronically.

3. <u>False</u>   The President of the company needs to prepare the annual report.

4. <u>True</u>   The head of sales and marketing wants to create a list of customer names, addresses, and buying preferences for use in targeted mailings.

Activity 1-3

1. In the data table given below, circle and label an example of each of the following elements.

   _B_ field   _A_ record

   _C_ value

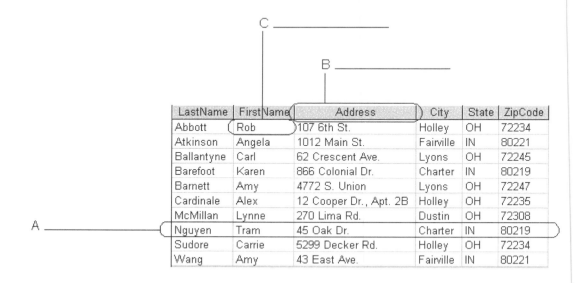

Activity 1-4

4. **What is this view of the data called?**

   Datasheet view.

   What fields of data are included in this table?

   The last and first name of each employee, along with the employee's ID and department number.

6. **How might you use this form?**

   It can be used to view and edit existing data and to add new records to the database.

8. **What information is given in this report?**

   This report shows a list of the employees in each department and an inventory of their computers.

10. **What data does this query provide?**

    It displays a datasheet of people in the Administration department, with employee names in alphabetical order.

12. **Match the type of Access object with the description of the function(s) that it performs.**

_b_	report	a.	Display data for editing.
_d_	table	b.	Arrange data for printed output.
_c_	query	c.	Display selected data.
_a_	form	d.	Store data on a single topic.

14. **What do you use the Relationships window for?**

It is where you define the relationships between the tables in your database.

Activity 1-5

2. **What are the types of information the database will store?**

Information on assets and their depreciation and maintenance histories, and information about employees, departments, and vendors.

Activity 1-6

4. **Are the fields in this database a match for the data you want to track?**

Answers will vary The database may contain more or different kinds of data than you need to record.

Lesson 2

Activity 2-1

1. **Given the preceding scenario, write a statement of purpose for the new database.**

Answers will vary somewhat but should be something like "The database will hold information on the company's inventory of computers and their assignment to employees."

Activity 2-2

1. **Given the statement of purpose and the existing data shown in Figure 2-2, list the fields you think you will need to include in the database.**

The list of fields may vary slightly, but should include:
- *Employee name*
- *Date received*
- *Employee department*
- *Asset tag number*
- *Description or manufacturer and description or note*

Activity 2-3

1. **Given the scenario above, list any additional fields you will need in the database.**

    Answers will vary slightly, but students should add:
    - *Warranty coverage*
    - *Purchase price*

Activity 2-4

1. **Using the previous field list and following the guidelines on naming fields and tables, list the tables you'll need with the fields that each will contain.**

    Answers will vary, but, at minimum, students should list the following tables with the fields indicated.

Activity 2-5

1. **What field does not contain the smallest meaningful values?**

    The Address field contains too much information.

    Why would this be a data maintenance problem?

    It would be difficult to query for addresses in a specific state, and you would not be able to sort them by zip code.

    What change to the table design should you make to correct this problem?

    Add additional fields to hold the City, State, and ZipCode data.

2. **What data normalization principle does this table violate?**

    There are repeated groups of fields.

    Why would this be a data maintenance problem?

    It would be difficult to total the amount of time devoted to a specific project. Also, if a single person was assigned to a third project, you would have to add two more fields to the table.

    In the space below, enter the sample data as it would be displayed in a properly designed table.

    The table should have a single Project field and a single Time field. The resulting sample data would appear as shown in the following graphic.

LastName	FirstName	Project	Time
Abbott	Rob	AA-765	45%
Abbott	Rob	QC-344	25%
Ballantyne	Carl	TS-1001	60%
Ballantyne	Carl	AA-699	15%
Barefoot	Karen	QC-344	80%
Sudore	Carrie	EN-29	20%
Sudore	Carrie	QC-405	65%
Wang	Amy	AA-780	30%

3. **What field contains unnecessarily repeated values?**

The Phone field.

What data maintenance problem does this cause?

You would have to edit phone numbers in more than one record.

What tables would you need to eliminate the repeated values in the Phone field?

One table containing the ProjectNumber, ProjectTitle, and ProjectManager fields, and another table containing ProjectManager and Phone fields.

4. **What field contains missing values?**

The Spouse field.

What data normalization principle does this violate?

That all fields in a table pertain to every record.

What tables would eliminate the blank values?

One table about Employees containing the EmployeeID and the name and address fields, and another table about spouses containing EmployeeID and Spouse fields.

Activity 2-6

1. **Examine the Employees table. In the space below, make notes on the changes you think should be made to the design of this table to meet the data normalization guidelines?**

The Name field should be broken into LastName and FirstName fields so each field will hold the smallest meaningful value.

Since the Department field holds repeated values, a Departments table should hold those values.

2. **Now examine the Computers table. List below the changes that should be made to the design.**

Since the Manufacturer name is repeated, there should be a Manufacturers table with ManufacturerID and Manufacturer (or ManufacturerName) fields. The ManufacturerID field could then be added to the Computers table to connect the data.

Since not all records have an entry in the Note field, that information belongs in a separate table containing the AssetTag field (to connect the data) and the Note field.

Activity 2-7

1. **What field or fields in the Employees table could serve as the primary key?**

The combination of the LastName and FirstName fields could potentially be the primary key, but, because it would be possible for two employees to have the same name, that would not be a good choice. The best primary key would be an EmployeeID field. If the company does not assign an identifier to each employee, the database designer could assign a unique number.

2. **In the Departments table, what field could be the primary key?**

   The DeptCode field should be the primary key. The values might be a department number or abbreviation unique to each department.

3. **What about the Computers table?**

   It's safe to assume that the AssetTag field would contain a unique value for each record and could be used as the primary key.

4. **What would be the primary keys for the Manufacturers and the Notes tables?**

   The ManufacturerID field would be the primary key of the Manufacturers table. The AssetTag field would be the primary key of the Notes table.

5. **Now you need to make sure that you have the foreign keys necessary to connect related data held in separate tables. How will you relate the data in the Employees and Departments tables?**

   The DeptCode field can be used. It is the primary key of the Departments table and can serve as the foreign key in the Employees tables.

6. **How will you be able to relate a particular computer to a particular employee?**

   A foreign key field of EmployeeID should be added to the Computers table.

7. **What field will relate the data in the Manufacturers and Computers tables?**

   The ManufacturerID field is the foreign key in the Computers table and can be connected to the ManufacturerID primary key field in the Manufacturers table.

8. **How will you associate a Note with a particular computer?**

   The AssetTag field is the primary key in both the Notes and Computers tables and will serve to connect the data.

Activity 2-8

1. **Examine the data in the Departments and Employees tables. What type of relationship exists between these tables?**

   A one-to-many relationship. Each employee can be in only one department, but each department can have many employees.

   How should you indicate this relationship in the database diagram?

   Draw a line from the DeptCode field in the Employees table to the DeptCode field in the Departments table. Mark a N at the Employees table end of the line and a 1 at the Departments table end of the line.

2. **What is the relationship between the Manufacturers and Computers tables?**

   One-to-many. Each computer is made by one manufacturer, but each manufacturer has supplied many computers.

3. **Now examine the data in the Computers and Notes tables. What is the relationship?**

   One-to-one. Each note relates to only one computer. Each computer has no more than one note associated with it.

4. **The last set of related tables is Employees and Computers. What is that relationship?**

   From the sample data, you can see that each employee can have more than one computer and each computer is assigned to only one employee. There is a one-to-many relationship between the Employees and Computers tables.

5. **Did your review of the relationships between the tables reveal any many-to-many relationships?**

   No, so no additional tables are needed to resolve them.

6. **Does your completed diagram resemble the one above?**

   See graphic.

Lesson 3

Activity 3-3

1. **What difference do you notice in the column headings?**

   There are spaces in the Employee ID, First Name, and Last Name column headings and no space in the DeptCode heading—which is exactly how you entered it.

Lesson 7

Activity 7-1

2. **What features does the printed datasheet have?**

   The name of the data source and the current date would be printed at the top of each page. The column headings would also be printed. The data is easy to read with each record arranged horizontally in a grid.

   What disadvantages are there to printing the query datasheet?

   The data is split across two pages.

5. **How does the AutoReport compare to the printed datasheet?**

   The fields are arranged in a vertical column. An extra blank line separates each record. There's no heading, date, or page numbers. The report is eight pages long.

Activity 7-2

11. **What are some of the features of the report?**

    Answers will depend on the report layout and style the student selected, but may include:

    - *A report title on the first page*

SOLUTIONS

- *A variety of fonts*
- *A variety of font colors*
- *Vertical lines dividing areas of data*
- *A footer containing the current date and page numbers*

Activity 7-3

2. **What information is in the Report Header and when does it print?**

The title and a function for the current date that prints once at the beginning of the report.

What information is contained in the Detail section?

The fields that will print for every record included in the report.

And what about the page footer?

It contains the page numbers and will print at the bottom of every page.

4. **How could you characterize the contents of the types of controls found in this report?**

Label controls contain descriptive text such as headings and labels. Text boxes contain data fields or functions.

Activity 7-7

6. **Why are these settings causing the blank pages?**

The report is in Portrait orientation, which means the page is 8.5 inches wide. The report width of 6.75 inches plus 1 inch left and right margins exceeds this width and causes the blank pages.

What do you think your options might be for fixing this problem?

You could:

- *Decrease the width of the lines and then decrease the width of the report in Design view.*
- *Change the report to Landscape orientation.*
- *Make the margins smaller.*

GLOSSARY

AutoNumber field
A field in which Access automatically enters a sequential and unique number, starting with a value of 1.

database
A collection of related information or data.

Datasheet view
The default view of data from a table or a query with the data arranged in rows and in columns.

denormalize
Combine data into one table that the normalization process indicated should be in two tables.

field
A category of information that pertains to all records.

foreign key field
A field used to connect related data in separate tables.

form
The Access object that enables you to view, enter, and edit data in a format similar to a paper form.

normalization
Reviewing data for possible maintenance problems.

object
A component of an Access database.

primary key
A field or combination of fields that contains a value that uniquely identifies a record.

query
The Access object that retrieves specific fields and/or records from one or more tables.

record
A set of data about one person or thing.

referential integrity
Guarding against accidental deletion of or changes to data that would invalidate the relationship between tables.

relational database
A database in which the data is stored in a structure of rows and columns.

report
The Access object that enables you to arrange data in a format suitable for printing.

select query
Query that retrieves data from one or more tables and enables you to ask questions about the data.

Switchboard
A form containing command buttons that enable the user to access the various objects in the database.

Tab order
The order in which values in a form are selected when you press [Tab].

table
A group of records stored in rows and columns.

task pane
Displays options for common Access functions on the right side of the screen.

templates
Provide a database designed to hold a certain type of data on which you can base a new database.

value
A single piece of data.

INDEX

task panes, 11
templates, 11
  creating a database, 10, 12
Text fields, 50
titles, 11
Toolbox
  creating new controls, 139
Total row, 99

V
values, 5

W
wizards, 46, 47, 108
  creating a form, 107, 109
  creating a query, 79, 80
  deciding on good form design, 111
  setting the primary key, 47

Z
Zoom box, 95

NOTES